California Bar Examination

Performance Tests and Selected Answers

July 2016

The State Bar Of California
Committee of Bar Examiners/Office of Admissions

180 Howard Street • San Francisco, CA 94105-1639 • (415) 538-2300
845 S. Figueroa Street • Los Angeles, CA 90017-2515 • (213) 765-1500

PERFORMANCE TESTS AND SELECTED ANSWERS

JULY 2016

CALIFORNIA BAR EXAMINATION

This publication contains two performance tests from the July 2016 California Bar Examination and two selected answers for each test.

The answers were assigned high grades and were written by applicants who passed the examination after one read. The answers were produced as submitted by the applicant, except that minor corrections in spelling and punctuation were made for ease in reading. They are reproduced here with the consent of the authors.

CONTENTS

July 2016

California
Bar
Examination

Performance Test A
INSTRUCTIONS AND FILE

IN RE POTENTIAL WILDOMAR PROPERTY LITIGATION

IN RE POTENTIAL WILDOMAR PROPERTY LITIGATION

INSTRUCTIONS

1. This performance test is designed to evaluate your ability to handle a select number of legal authorities in the context of a factual problem involving a client.

2. The problem is set in the fictional State of Columbia, one of the United States.

3. You will have two sets of materials with which to work: a File and a Library.

4. The File contains factual materials about your case. The first document is a memorandum containing the instructions for the tasks you are to complete.

5. The Library contains the legal authorities needed to complete the tasks. The case reports may be real, modified, or written solely for the purpose of this performance test. If the cases appear familiar to you, do not assume that they are precisely the same as you have read before. Read each thoroughly, as if it were new to you. You should assume that cases were decided in the jurisdictions and on the dates shown. In citing cases from the Library, you may use abbreviations and omit page citations.

6. You should concentrate on the materials provided, but you should also bring to bear on the problem your general knowledge of the law. What you have learned in law school and elsewhere provides the general background for analyzing the problem; the File and Library provide the specific materials with which you must work.

7. Although there are no parameters on how to apportion your time, you should allow yourself sufficient time to thoroughly review the materials and organize your planned response.

8. Your response will be graded on its compliance with instructions and on its content, thoroughness, and organization.

OFFICE OF THE COUNTY COUNSEL

COUNTY OF RIVERDALE

15000 CIVIC CENTER WAY

DIXON, COLUMBIA

TO: Applicant

FROM: Charles Drumm, Assistant County Counsel

DATE: July 26, 2016

RE: Potential Wildomar Property Litigation

We represent the Riverdale Regional Park District in this matter and our client contact is Pamela Walls, the District's General Manager.

The District has received a letter from counsel for Geraldine Santa Maria threatening litigation over the District's intended conveyance by sale to the City of Dixon of a parcel of land referred to as the "Wildomar Property."

It is the District's position that, under the Columbia Regional Park District Act ("Act"), real property is "actually dedicated" by a district, and thereby becomes subject to a requirement that it may validly be conveyed only with voter consent, only if the district's board of directors adopts a resolution dedicating the property. The District's Board of Directors never adopted a resolution dedicating the Wildomar Property, and accordingly never sought or obtained voter consent for its conveyance.

Santa Maria's position, in contrast, is that, under the Act, real property is "actually dedicated" simply by virtue of its acquisition.

Santa Maria is an environmental activist who has brought numerous lawsuits against small local public entities whom she believes have violated the law.

General Manager Walls is determined that Santa Maria will not prevail against the District.

Please draft a letter for my signature in response to Santa Maria's counsel's letter. In the letter, be sure to show:

(1) that the District's position that it may validly convey the Wildomar Property without satisfying the Act's voter-consent requirement is sound under the facts and the law;

and

(2) that Santa Maria's contrary position is unsound.

Begin the letter with a statement of the District's position and end the letter with a statement that the District will go forward with the conveyance notwithstanding the threatened litigation.

In drafting the letter, you should address all of the legal issues, preparing headings to separate your discussion of the District's position and Santa Maria's contrary position into distinct parts. You should use the facts persuasively in setting out the legal analysis, but you should not prepare a separate statement of facts. Finally, you should emphasize the law and facts supportive of the District's position, but you should also address and deal with any law or facts supportive of Santa Maria's position.

STANDISH & LOBERT LLP
ATTORNEYS AT LAW
1616 OAK STREET
DIXON, COLUMBIA

July 22, 2016

Pamela Walls

General Manager

Riverdale Regional Park District

1000 Independence Avenue

Dixon, Columbia

Re: Intended Conveyance of Wildomar Property

Dear Ms. Walls:

We have been retained by Geraldine Santa Maria, who is a resident of the Riverdale Regional Park District ("District"), to challenge the District's intended conveyance of the Wildomar Property ("Property") by sale to the City of Dixon ("City").

Under Section 40 of the Columbia Regional Park District Act ("Act"), a regional park district "may not validly convey any interest in any real property … without the consent of a majority of the voters of the district voting at a special election called by the board and held for that purpose" if that interest has been "actually dedicated and used for park purposes." Under the common law, a real property interest may be "dedicated" by an offer by a private owner, and an acceptance by a public entity, having the character of a gift as well as a contract. *See Baldwin v. City of Lake Alston* (Colum. Supreme Ct. 1999). But under Section 65 of the Act, a real property interest is "dedicated" by a regional park district simply by acquisition: "The legal title to all property acquired by the district under the provisions of this Act ... is *dedicated* ... for ... the uses and purposes set forth in this Act ...." (Italics added).

It is indisputable that the Property has been "actually dedicated and used" so as to subject the District to the voter-consent requirement of Section 40, mandating that it must obtain the "consent of a majority of the voters of the district voting at a special election" before it may "validly convey" the Property.

As for "actual use," the Property, although not developed into a regional park, has nevertheless functioned as such.

As for "actual dedication," the matter is similar. To begin with, the Property has been "dedicated" under the common law. Separately and independently, the Property has been "dedicated" under Section 65.

Further, it is undisputed that the District has not satisfied the voter-consent requirement of Section 40, having failed even to seek the "consent of a majority of the voters of the district voting at a special election" for the conveyance of the Property.

As a consequence, because it is indisputable that the Property has been "actually dedicated" so as to subject the District to the voter-consent requirement of Section 40, and because it is likewise undisputed that the District has not satisfied that requirement, the District may not "validly convey" the Property.

We are aware that it is the District's position that, under Section 40, a real property interest is "actually dedicated" by a district so as to trigger the voter-consent requirement only by the "adoption of a resolution by [the district's] board of directors" dedicating the interest, and not simply by virtue of acquiring the interest under Section 65. The District's position, however, is specious.

It is plain that "actually dedicated" in Section 40 and "dedicated" in Section 65 are identical. Indeed, unless "dedicated" in Section 65 were read as identical to "actually dedicated" in Section 40, Section 65 would be rendered meaningless.

Moreover, although the adoption of a resolution by a district's board of directors is an *alternative* method of "actual dedication" for an "easement" under Section 40 *in addition to* simple "acquisition" under Section 65, it is *not* a method of "actual dedication," additional or otherwise, for "any other" real property interest.

On August 1, 2016, we will file an appropriate action, on Ms. Santa Maria's behalf, to prohibit the District from going forward with the intended conveyance of the Property to the City unless and until it satisfies the voter-consent requirement of Section 40.

As you are doubtless aware, over the years, Ms. Santa Maria has found it necessary to file several actions against various local public entities to compel them to comply with the law. As you are also doubtless aware, she has prevailed in all of those actions, either by settlement or by judgment. She is confident that she will prevail in any action that the District may force her to file.

Accordingly, should the District wish to respond to this letter in an attempt to render Ms. Santa Maria's coming action unnecessary—and in an effort to avoid incurring attorney's fees and related expenses that the District can ill afford in the current economic climate—we request that the District respond expeditiously. We wish to make Ms. Santa Maria's position clear: The only response by the District that will obviate her coming action is its formal and binding commitment not to proceed with the intended conveyance of the Property without voter consent.

Very truly yours,

Michael Standish

Michael Standish

SUBMISSION TO THE BOARD OF DIRECTORS
RIVERDALE REGIONAL PARK DISTRICT

From: Patricia Smith, General Manager

Date: June 5, 1995

Re: Purchase of Real Property, Wildomar

I recommend that the Board of Directors adopt a motion to the following effect:

1.   Accept and execute the Agreement for Purchase of Real Property for 161.27 acres of real property in Wildomar, Columbia, identified as APN 362-180-004 ("Property"), from Lucille Potts;

2.   Direct the Administrative Office to transfer $980,000 for the purchase of the Property;

3.   Approve the expenditure of $950,000 for the acquisition of the Property and $30,000 for escrow fees and related costs;

4.   Authorize the District to accept as a gift the difference between the appraised value of the Property, $1,370,000, and the purchase price of the Property, $950,000, amounting to $420,000;

5.   Authorize the District to administer all necessary and appropriate documents to complete the purchase of the Property; and

6.   Direct the Clerk of the Board to take all ministerial actions necessary and appropriate to complete the purchase of the Property.

MINUTES OF THE BOARD OF DIRECTORS
RIVERDALE REGIONAL PARK DISTRICT

On motion of Director Cisneros, seconded by Director Mullen and duly carried by unanimous vote, IT WAS ORDERED that the motion recommended by General Manager Smith, dated June 5, 1995, entitled "Purchase of Real Property, Wildomar," is adopted as recommended.

Ayes: Buster, Taglieri, Cisneros, Wilson, and Mullen

Noes: None

Abstain: None

Absent: None

Date: June 12, 1995

Gerald A. Maloney
Clerk of the Board

By ___Laura Soto_____
      Deputy

THE BOARD OF DIRECTORS
RIVERDALE REGIONAL PARK DISTRICT
RESOLUTION NO. 1995-165
AUTHORIZING PURCHASE OF REAL PROPERTY

BE IT RESOLVED by the Board of Directors of the Riverdale Regional Park District, State of Columbia, in regular session assembled on July 18, 1995, that the purchase of 161.27 acres of real property in Wildomar, Columbia, identified as APN 362-180-004, from Lucille Potts for the sum of $950,000, is approved, and the General Manager is authorized and directed to take the necessary and appropriate action to complete the purchase, including obtaining funds to pay the purchase price and the costs and expenses of the acquisition.

ROLL CALL:

Ayes: Buster, Taglieri, Cisneros, Wilson, and Mullen

Noes: None

Abstain: None

Absent: None

The foregoing is certified to be a true copy of a resolution duly adopted by said Board of Directors on the date therein set forth.

Gerald A. Maloney
Clerk of the Board

By _____*Laura Soto*_____
        Deputy

AGREEMENT FOR PURCHASE OF REAL PROPERTY

Agreement dated this 19th day of July 1995, by and between Lucille Potts, hereinafter "Seller," and the Riverdale Regional Park District, hereinafter "Buyer."

1. The Property.

Seller and Buyer agree that Seller will sell and Buyer will buy 161.27 acres of real property in Wildomar, Columbia, identified as APN 362-180-004 ("Property").

2. Purchase Price.

The total purchase price to be paid by Buyer for the Property will be $950,000.

3. Gift.

Buyer accepts as a gift from Seller the difference between the appraised value of the Property, $1,370,000, and the purchase price of the Property, $950,000, amounting to $420,000.

4. Closing.

Closing will be held be on or about July 20, 1995, at a time and place designated by Buyer. Buyer shall choose the escrow, title and/or closing agent. Seller agrees to convey tille by a deed.

__*Lucille Potts*_____
Lucille Potts

__*Patricia Smith* _____
Riverdale Regional Park District

GRANT DEED

FOR VALUABLE CONSIDERATION, receipt of which is hereby acknowledged, Lucille Potts GRANTS to the Riverdale Regional Park District, State of Columbia, the 161.27 acres of real property in Wildomar, Columbia, identified as APN 362-180-004, for park purposes in perpetuity.

Dated: July 20, 1995

By _____*Lucille Potts*_____
        Lucille Potts

THE BOARD OF DIRECTORS
RIVERDALE REGIONAL PARK DISTRICT
RESOLUTION NO. 2016-210
NOTICE OF INTENT TO CONVEY REAL PROPERTY BY SALE

WHEREAS the Riverdale Regional Park District, State of Columbia, acquired 161.27 acres of real property in Wildomar, Columbia, identified as APN 362-180-004 ("Property"), in 1995 with the hope of developing it into a regional park;

WHEREAS the Riverdale Regional Park District has been unsuccessful in obtaining the funds necessary to develop the Property into a regional park;

WHEREAS the Property has given rise to health and safety problems as the public has continued to frequent it without parking and restroom and other facilities;

BE IT RESOLVED by the Board of Directors of the Riverdale Regional Park District, in regular session assembled on July 14, 2016, and NOTICE IS HEREBY GIVEN pursuant to Section 63 of the Columbia Regional Park District Act, that this Board intends to convey the Property by sale, on or after 9:00 a.m. on August 15, 2016, to the City of Dixon for the sum of $2,100,000.

BE IT FURTHER RESOLVED by the Board of Directors of the Riverdale Regional Park District, that this Board may validly convey the Property to the City of Dixon without the consent of a majority of the voters of this District voting at a special election called by this Board and held for that purpose because this Board has not "actually dedicated and used" the Property, within the meaning of Section 40 of the Columbia Regional Park District Act, because it never adopted a resolution dedicating the Property and never developed the Property.

ROLL CALL:

Ayes: Kim, Brady, Horstman, Chen, and Peters

Noes: None

Abstain: None

Absent: None

The foregoing is certified to be a true copy of a resolution duly adopted by said Board of Directors on the date therein set forth.

Myra R. Taylor
Clerk of the Board

By ____Robert Gupta_____
        Deputy

DIXON *DAILY NEWS*

FRIDAY, JULY 15, 2016

"Wildomar Regional Park—Now You See It, Now You Don't"

Since 1995, the sign posted at the end of Clayton Road promised, "The Future Site of Wildomar Regional Park." Now, it appears, the promise will not be kept.

Last night, the Board of Directors of the Riverdale Regional Park District voted to issue a notice of its intent to sell the 160+-acre parcel at the end of Clayton Road to the City of Dixon. The district had purchased the property in 1995 for less than $1 million, had never developed it, and is now selling it for more than twice as much.

District General Manager Pamela Walls and Dixon Mayor David Stokovich both expressed satisfaction that the deal, which had been negotiated in fits and starts over more than a year, was finally nearing completion. Stokovich stated that Dixon had long been seeking a location for a new community college campus to accommodate its growing population. "The property," he said, "is beautiful and, what's more, it's ideally suited to our needs." For her part, Walls stated that the district decided that the time had come to sell it. "We bought it in 1995," she said, "hoping to develop it into a regional park with athletic facilities for games, trails for running and hiking and, of course, open space simply for enjoying. It turned out, however, the funds for development never materialized. The sale will give us funds we can use for our other regional parks." Stokovich added, "It's a win for everyone."

But everyone does not agree. The property has long been popular with hikers, hunters, and birdwatchers because of its pristine beauty. Its former owner, Lucille Potts, never developed the land and never posted it to keep the public out, and neither did the district. As a result, hikers, hunters, and especially birdwatchers have continuously flocked to it. Geraldine Santa Maria, a local environmental activist who lives adjacent to the property, spoke out strongly against the sale at last night's meeting of the district's board of directors. She argued unsuccessfully that the board could not go ahead with the sale because it had not obtained the consent of the district's voters and was "just trying to make a quick buck." Questioned as she left the meeting, she stated that she would consider litigation unless the board were to change its mind.

District General Manager Walls did not discount the possibility of a lawsuit, but expressed confidence that the district would prevail if it were to find itself in court. "It's true we haven't obtained voter consent for the sale," she said, "but that's because we don't have to."

As for the "broken promise" of Wildomar Regional Park, Walls just shook her head. She denied that the board "was in it for the money." She went on: "Although the community college campus won't be a regional park, it'll have athletic facilities, trails, and open space, the kind of things we had hoped for. It's not perfect, but it's close enough." Whether the district's residents—including Santa Maria—agree, only time will tell.

July 2016

California
Bar
Examination

Performance Test A
LIBRARY

IN RE POTENTIAL WILDOMAR PROPERTY LITIGATION

LIBRARY

Osuna on Real Property, Dedication (5th Ed. 1995)...

**Selected Provisions of the
Columbia Regional Park District Act**..

Teller Irrigation District v. Collins
Columbia Supreme Court (1988) ....

Baldwin v. City of Lake Alston
Columbia Supreme Court (1999) ....

Dedication

Section 1. Introduction

Dedication Defined. Generally speaking, dedication is the application of private real property to a public use by the acts of its owner and a public entity. Any real property interest may be dedicated.

Kinds of Dedication. The two kinds of dedication are statutory dedication and common law dedication.

Statutory Dedication. Dedication is generally governed by statute. Statutory dedication is accomplished through compliance with the requirements specified by the statute in question, such as by the recordation of a map in substantial compliance with the Subdivision Map Act.

Common Law Dedication. Dedication in the absence of a statute is available under the common law. Normally, common law dedication does not involve any payment by the public entity to the private property owner and hence partakes of the character of a gift. Common law dedication entails, in substance, an offer by a private owner, and an acceptance by a public entity, of real property subject to a specified restricted public use in perpetuity. Common law dedication may be either express or implied. Accordingly, common law dedication may be found whenever there is a basis for finding an offer, either express or implied, by the property owner to give the property for perpetual public use, and an acceptance, either express or implied, by the public entity to receive the property for the same use. Although common law dedication therefore takes on the character of a contract, it does not lose any character it may have as a gift.

*   *   *

SELECTED PROVISIONS OF THE
COLUMBIA REGIONAL PARK DISTRICT ACT

Section 1. Purpose

The purpose of the Act is to foster the creation and preservation of regional parks for the enjoyment of the public.

Section 2. District Defined

"District," as used in this Act, means any regional park district formed pursuant to this Act.

*   *   *

Section 27. Board of Directors

The government of each district shall be vested in a board of five directors. Directors shall be residents of the district.

The district may act only through its board of directors or through such officers, employees, or agents appointed by the board, subject to the authority the board confers upon any such officers, employees, or agents.

*   *   *

Section 40.   Powers; Acquisition; Conveyance of Property; Consent of Voters

A district may take by grant, appropriation, purchase, gift, devise, condemnation, or lease, and may hold, use, enjoy, and lease or dispose of real and personal property of every kind, and rights in real and personal property, within or without the district, necessary to the full exercise of its powers.

An easement or any other interest in real property may be actually dedicated for park purposes by the adoption of a resolution by the board of directors, and any interest so dedicated may be conveyed only as provided in this section.

A district may not validly convey any interest in any real property actually dedicated and used for park purposes without the consent of a majority of the voters of the district voting at a special election called by the board and held for that purpose.

*   *   *

Section 43. General Powers

A district may make contracts, employ labor, and do all acts necessary for the full exercise of its powers.

*   *   *

Section 47. Board of Directors; Mode of Action; Resolutions, Ordinances and Motions; Form and Requisites

The board of directors shall act only by ordinance, resolution, or a motion duly recorded in the minutes of the meeting. The ayes and noes shall be taken upon the passage of all ordinances or resolutions, and entered upon the journal of the proceedings of the board.

*   *   *

Section 63. Sale or Lease of Surplus Property; Disposition of Proceeds

If, in the opinion of the board, any real or personal property owned by the district, or any interest therein, becomes unnecessary for the purposes of the district, the board may, subject to the provisions of Section 40, sell such property, or interest therein. The proceeds of any sale of such property, or interest therein, shall be used for and applied to such purposes of the district as the board may, by resolution, determine.

*   *   *

Section 65. Property; Title to Vest in District

The legal title to all property acquired by the district under the provisions of this Act shall immediately and by operation of law vest in the district, and shall be held by the district in trust for, and is dedicated and set apart for, the uses and purposes set forth in this Act. The board may hold, use, acquire, manage, occupy, and possess such property, as provided in this Act.

*   *   *

TELLER IRRIGATION DISTRICT v. COLLINS
Columbia Supreme Court (1988)

Phyllis Mosier recovered a judgment against the Teller Irrigation District (District), a public entity created pursuant to the Columbia Irrigation District Act (Act), for damages the District caused by its negligence in flooding her land. The District, however, refused to satisfy the judgment. Mosier caused execution to issue on the judgment, directing Charles Collins, the Sheriff of Teller County, to levy upon and sell so much of the District's real and/or personal property as was necessary to satisfy the judgment.

The District then brought this action to restrain Sheriff Collins from levying upon and selling any of its property. The trial court refused to restrain Sheriff Collins and rendered judgment against the District. The District appealed.

It cannot be doubted that it was the duty of the District to satisfy Mosier's judgment. But the question here is whether the performance of that duty may be compelled by an execution, levy, and sale of the District's property.

All of the property owned by the District, both real and personal, was acquired by virtue of Section 13 of the Act, which declares that the "legal title to all property acquired under the provisions of this Act shall immediately and by operation of law vest in the district, and shall be held by the district in trust for and is hereby dedicated and set apart to the uses and purposes set forth in this Act"—that is, for irrigation.

Under Section 13 of the Act, the "legal title" to *all* of the District's property is held "in trust" by the District and "is dedicated and set apart to the uses and purposes" specified, namely, irrigation.

Section 13 of the Act is similar to analogous provisions in dozens of analogous statutes creating districts—e.g., Section 34 of the Columbia Water Reclamation District Act and Section 65 of the Columbia Regional Park District Act. Such provisions have been held to create a public trust over all of the district's property, with the district itself as the owner of the legal title, the residents of the district as the owners of the beneficial title, and the district's board of directors as the trustees. *Merchants' Bank v. Erickson Irrigation Dist.* (Colum. Ct. App. 1976). Public trusts have long been exempted from execution, levy, and sale, not because districts and their boards are considered incapable of wrongdoing, but solely to protect the districts' residents. *Sannerville v. Itsell* (Colum. Supreme Ct. 1880).

Therefore, Section 13 of the Act creates a public trust over all of the District's property, and the public trust so created is exempt from execution, levy, and sale.

We are not unaware that the District has come to court seeking equity in spite of its failure to do equity. But however blameworthy the District may be in refusing to satisfy Mosier's judgment, it cannot be estopped from insisting that property that is in public trust and, as such, is exempted from execution, levy, and sale, must remain so for the protection of its residents.

Reversed.

BALDWIN v. CITY OF LAKE ALSTON
Columbia Supreme Court (1999)

The trial court entered a judgment granting a petition for writ of mandate by Skip Baldwin, a resident of the City of Lake Alston, in which Baldwin challenged the City's adoption of an ordinance providing for the sale of a seven-acre parcel of real property—the so-called Woodside Lot—to Human Habitat, a non-profit corporation, for use in constructing affordable housing. The judgment determined that, by an ordinance adopted years earlier, the City had dedicated the Woodside Lot to "public recreation purposes," and had thereby deprived itself of the power to put the lot to any other use. The City appealed. We reverse.

In 1976, the South Plains Railroad Company proposed donation of the Woodside Lot to the City "for public recreation purposes," "conditioned upon the City assuming the responsibility for removing rails and restoring streets where railroad tracks have previously been retired." The City's Department of Recreation and Parks issued a report to the City Council, in which it noted that the lot had an estimated value of $600,000 and that the total cost of removing tracks and restoring streets would total about $200,000; it stated that acquisition of the lot would be profitable to the City; and it recommended that if the City Council were inclined to accept the lot, it should refer the matter to the City Attorney to work out the terms of an agreement with South Plains because "there may be legal problems relating to removal of the tracks and restoration of the streets ...."

In 1977, the City Council adopted Ordinance No. 1977-149. The ordinance provided that the City may "accept donation" of the Woodside Lot "upon payment by the South Plains Railroad Company of $200,000." South Plains sent a letter to the City Council, enclosing a conditional donation deed for the lot "for public recreation purposes." The letter stated that "Delivery of this instrument is conditioned upon receipt of a Certified Copy of the Resolution adopted by the City Council of the City of Lake Alston, accepting the Donation Deed." The letter concluded that it was with pleasure that South Plains was able to "donate" the lot "for public recreation purposes."

Between 1977 and 1979, the City apparently did nothing to respond to South Plains' letter.

In 1980, in the course of routine review of files, the City Attorney discovered the unresponded-to South Plains letter. The City Attorney went on to discover that South Plains had not made the $200,000 payment required by Ordinance No. 1977-149. The City Attorney sent a letter to South Plains inquiring about the $200,000 payment. This time, it was South Plains that failed to respond.

In 1983, after the City had levied an assessment of about $20,000 on the Woodside Lot and sought payment from South Plains, South Plains delivered an unconditional donation deed and the City excused payment of the assessment. The City did not request, and South Plains did not make, the $200,000 payment required by Ordinance No. 1977-149.

Between 1983 and 1995, the City used the Woodside Lot for public recreation purposes.

In 1996, following a series of City Council hearings on the need for affordable housing in the general vicinity of the Woodside Lot, the City sold the lot to Human Habitat to construct such housing.

Immediately thereafter, Baldwin filed a petition for writ of mandate challenging the sale of the Woodside Lot.

The sole issue on appeal is whether the City had dedicated the Woodside Lot to "public recreation purposes," and had thereby deprived itself of the power to put the lot to any other use. That issue depends on whether the lot can be deemed to have been dedicated under the common law by force of Ordinance No. 1977-149.

"Common law dedication entails ... an offer by a private owner, and an acceptance by a public entity, of real property subject to a specified restricted public use in perpetuity"; it "may be either express or implied"; and it may have the character of a "gift" as well as a "contract." *Osuna on Real Property*, Dedication, Section 1 (5th Ed. 1995). Therefore, unless the private owner's offer is accepted by the public entity, there is no dedication of the property and hence no restriction on its use.

Cities are required to enact ordinances to enable the making of contracts for the acquisition and disposition of real property. *American-Hawaiian Steamship Co. v. Home Sav. and Loan Assn.* (Colum. Ct. App. 1974).

The rules for the construction of statutes apply equally to ordinances and other municipal measures. *Terminal Plaza Corp. v. City of St. Francis* (Colum. Ct. App. 1986). Under these rules, courts should read the provision in question according to its plain language. *Ibid.* In addition, courts should *not* read the provision in such a way as to render any part surplusage. *Ibid.* And courts should read a provision authorizing particular action by particular means as *discretionary* for the *action* but *mandatory* for the *means. Ibid.*

The City of Lake Alston City Charter provides that the "City Council may make any contract for the acquisition and/or disposition of any real property or any interest in real property, as it may deem necessary and proper, by enacting an ordinance." City of Lake Alston Munic. Charter, Section 73. Under the provision quoted, the City Council may choose to make any real property contract it wishes, but must make it by ordinance.

After review, we conclude that the Woodside Lot cannot be deemed to have been dedicated under the common law by force of Ordinance No. 1977-149. Although South Plains may have *offered* the lot under a perpetual restriction, the City did not *accept* it under that restriction. The ordinance states in plain language, which can hardly be treated as surplusage, that the City may "accept donation" of the Woodside Lot for public recreation purposes—but only "upon payment by the South Plains Railroad Company of $200,000." The ordinance's language can reasonably be interpreted only as an acceptance of the "donation" conditioned on South Plains' payment of $200,000 payment. That condition, however, was never satisfied.

The trial court accordingly erred when it concluded that the City had dedicated the Woodside Lot to "public recreation purposes."

Reversed.

PT-A: SELECTED ANSWER 1

July 26, 2016

Standish & Lobert LLP
1616 Oak Street
Dixon, Columbia

To Mr. Michael Standish:

We have received your letter setting forth your client's position, and we respectfully disagree. Based on our research, our position is that, under the Columbia Regional Park District Act ("Act" or "CRPDA"), real property is "actually dedicated" by a district, and thereby becomes subject to the requirement that it may validly be conveyed only with voter consent, only if the district's board of directors adopts a resolution dedicating the property. Because the District's Board of Directors never adopted a resolution dedicating the Wildomar Property, that property was never actually dedicated and the District did not need to obtain voter consent for its conveyance.

The District May Validly Convey the Wildomar Property Without Satisfying the Act's Voter-Consent Requirement

The District may validly convey the Wildomar Property without voter-consent because it never actually dedicated it in the manner laid out in the Act.

The Columbia Regional Park District Act ("Act" or "CRPDA") was passed for the following purpose: "to foster the creation and preservation of regional parks for the enjoyment of the public." CRPDA § 1. The Act divides land in Columbia into districts that are each governed by a board of directors. CRPDA

§§ 2, 27. Section 40 of the Act states that a district may "hold, use, enjoy, or dispose of real and personal property of every kind . . . necessary to the full exercise of its powers." CRPDA § 40. This power is admittedly limited by the following provision that an "easement or any other interest in real property . . . [actually] dedicated may be conveyed only as provided in [Section 40]." *Id.* That is, once "actually dedicated," a district "may not validly convey any interest in any real property actually dedicated and used for park purposes without the consent of a majority of the voters of the district voting at a special election . . . ." *Id.* The question of whether the District may validly convey without voter consent turns, then, on whether there was actual dedication of the Wildomar Property.

Common Law Dedication Does Not Apply

The common law rules for dedication do not apply here. This is because the Act itself provides the means of dedication: an interest in real property "may be actually dedicated for park purposes by the adoption of a resolution by the board of directors." CRPDA § 40. This is the standard that applies. As the leading treatise on the subject noted, dedication is "generally governed by statute" and statutory dedication is accomplished through "compliance with the requirements specified by the statute in question." *Osuna on Real Property, Dedication § 1* (5th Ed. 1995). Common law dedication is available only "in the absence of a statute." *Id.*

There Is No Statutory Dedication

As mentioned above, the Act itself provides the means of dedication that applies here: an interest in real property "may be actually dedicated for park purposes by the adoption of a resolution by the board of directors." CRPDA § 40. When interpreting and applying statutes, the general rules for the construction of statutes applies. Courts should read the provision in question according to its plain language. *See Baldwin v. City of Lake Alston.* In addition, courts should *not* read the provision in such a way as to render any part surplusage. *Id.* And courts should read a provision authorizing particular action by particular means as discretionary for the action but mandatory for the means. *Id.*

If we apply these rules of construction to Section 40 of the Act, then its meaning becomes clear. The plain language of the statute states that actual dedication is accomplished by "the adoption of a resolution by the board of directors." If we are not to read the provision in such a way as to render any part surplusage, then adoption of a resolution has to be a necessary prerequisite to actual dedication. Otherwise, those words would have no effect and be mere surplusage. And considering that this provision is authorizing particular action (actual dedication of real property interests) by particular means (adopting a resolution), it should be understood that adopting a resolution is a mandatory means of actually dedicating a property interest.

Given that this is the meaning of Section 40 with respect to actual dedication, there was no actual dedication of the Wildomar Property. A review of the public records regarding the Wildomar Property uncovers, prior to the resolution to sell the property, only a single resolution adopted by the Board back on July 18, 1995. All that resolution did was approve the purchase of the Wildomar Property for $950,000 and empower the General Manager to take the necessary and appropriate action to complete the purchase. There was no language in that resolution "actually dedicating" the property. The later resolution to convey the property by sale also lacks any language referring to "actual dedication" other than to explicitly state that there was no "actual dedication" of the Wildomar Property.

And since there was no actual dedication of the property, the provision of Section 40 requiring voter consent to convey any interest in real property does not apply. The Board and the District may convey the Wildomar Property as it sees fit to further its statutory purpose.

Santa Maria's Contrary Position is Unsound

Your client makes a number of points but they are all unsound.

There Is a Difference Between "Actually Dedicated" and "Dedicated"

It is true that Section 65 of the Act states that "legal title to all property acquired by the district under the provisions of this Act . . . is dedicated and set apart for, the uses and purposes set forth in this Act." But as the Court in *Baldwin* stated, courts are not to read provisions of a statute in such a way as to render any part surplusage. *See Baldwin*. If a court were to interpret "actually dedicated" in Section 40 and "dedicated" in Section 65 to mean the same thing, then the language requiring adoption of a resolution by the board of directors would become surplusage. There would be no situation where a board would need to go through the process of adopting a resolution if simply acquiring the property automatically created "actual dedication." The only reading that makes sense is if "actual dedication" and "dedication" mean different things, and the fact that the legislature used the phrase "actually dedicated" in Section 40 but only used the word "dedicated" in Section 65 is indicative of the difference. Moreover, if all property became actually dedicated by acquisition, then the phrase in Section 40 providing that "any interest so dedicated may be conveyed only as provided in this section" has no meaning. This phrase suggests that there are other sections in the Act that also lay out means of conveying real property interests. But if all property acquired by the District is automatically dedicated, then they would all have to be conveyed as provided in Section 40 and those other sections would have no effect.

And contrary to your client's assertions, reading a difference between "actually dedicated" and "dedicated" would not render Section 65 meaningless.

What Section 65's "dedication" provision does is protect the District (and the public) from judgment creditors seeking to levy on lands dedicated and held in public trust. This can be inferred from the case of *Teller Irrigation District v. Collins*, where an individual sought to enforce a judgment against the Teller Irrigation District through a forced levy and sale. The Court held that, pursuant to Section 13 of the Columbia Irrigation District Act (which is equivalent to Section 65 of the Act in question here), legal title to real property acquired by the District is held in trust to the public and is exempt from forced sale. *Collins*. That is the kind of sale that Section 65 "dedication" is meant to prevent, and it is different in kind from the sale at issue here where the Board and the District are seeking to exercise their powers to sell the property for the benefit of their "trust" and their statutory purpose.

The "Actual Dedication" Provision in Section 40 Is Not Limited to Easements

Section 40 very specifically states that "[a]n easement *or any other interest in real property* may be actually dedicated for park purposes by the adoption of a resolution by the board of directors." CRPDA § 40 (emphasis added). Bringing the rules of construction to bear once again on this provision, it is plain that adoption of a resolution is a method to actually dedicate for both easements and any other interest. Any other reading would render the phrase "or any other interest in real property" into a nullity. In fact, your client reads in additional language that is nowhere in the statute by claiming that this is merely an "alternative" method of dedicating an easement.

There Was No Common Law Dedication

As mentioned above, the rules for common law dedication do not apply where there is an applicable statute. But even if the common law rule were to apply, there is no dedication here. Normally, common law dedication does not involve any payment by the public entity to the private property owner. *Osuna.* But the public records clearly show that the District paid the former owner of the Wildomar Property for the conveyance. Patricia Smith, the General Manager, first submitted a proposal that the Board spend $980,000 for the purchase of the property. The minutes of the June 12, 1995 Board meeting show that the Board unanimously approved the "Purchase" of the Wildomar Property. The Board adopted a resolution for the expenditure of $950,000 for the purchase of the property. And the final agreement between the District and the previous owner had a provision for the $950,000 purchase price.

Now it is true that these records also show that the District purchased the property at a discount, and the difference was considered to be a gift. But common law dedication entails, in substance, an offer by a private owner and an acceptance by a public entity of real property "subject to a specified restricted public use in perpetuity" that may be express or implied. *Osuna.* Again, a review of the public records concerning the original purchase of this property by the District does not indicate that it took the property subject to a specified restricted public use. Nowhere, from the original submission to the Board to the minutes of the Board meeting to the resolution to the final sale agreement, is there any express mention of a specified restricted use or any language that might imply such a restriction. The only document that contains any mention of a potential specified restricted public use is the grant deed which purported to convey the land "for park purposes in perpetuity." But absent any corroborating evidence to support it, such precatory language alone does not rise to the level of imposing a specified restricted use.

Moreover, as the Court in *Baldwin* held, there is no common law dedication where the grantor *offered* his land under a perpetual restriction but the grantee did not *accept* it under that restriction. *Baldwin.* While the final deed might have purported to convey the land with some language about using it for park purposes, there is no indication in the original dealings and the final sale agreement that showed the District *accepted* any such restriction.

Finally, the mere fact that the District and its Board operate under a statutory act whose express purpose is to foster the creation and preservation of regional parks does not automatically make every conveyance of land to it into a common law dedication by implication. If that were so, the District's powers to "dispose of real and personal property of every kind, and rights in real and personal property, within or without the district" would be rendered a nullity. It would also render a nullity the provision providing for the means of "actually dedicating" real property interests. As mentioned, a Board would never have a reason to adopt a resolution actually dedicating real property if all property it acquired was automatically dedicated under the common law.

There Was No Actual Use

In addition to the fact that there was no "actual dedication," and contrary to your client's assertions, there was no "actual use" of the property to trigger Section 40's prohibitions. Under Section 40, a district may not validly convey any interest in real property that is "actually dedicated *and used for park purposes*" without voter consent. CRPDA § 40 (emphasis added). Here, there has been no actual use of the Wildomar Property by the District. The Notice of Intent to Convey in the public records shows that the District has failed to obtain the funds necessary to develop the Wildomar Property into a regional park. There is no indication that the Board has acted in any way to put the Wildomar Property into any sort of use. The fact that members of the public might come onto the land to hike or hunt does not mean that *the District* has made actual use of the land. Members of the public have been coming onto the Wildomar Property to hike, hunt, and birdwatch even before the District purchased the land, back when it was still under the ownership of Lucille Potts. It cannot be the case that by simple inaction, the District has actually used the Wildomar Property.

Moreover, to interpret the general public's use of the land as actual use by the District would render portions of the Act mere surplusage. Section 27 of the Act states that the district may act only through its board of directors or through such officers, employees, or agents appointed by the board and subject to its authority. CRPDA § 27. Section 47 of the Act then states that the board of directors shall act only by ordinance, resolution, or a motion duly recorded in the minutes of the meeting. CRPDA § 47. Nothing in the public record indicates that the Board has so acted here, and it cannot be the case that the general public's actions can be imputed to the Board and the District contrary to the plain language of the Act.

--

In light of the above, the District intends to go forward with the conveyance notwithstanding your client's threatened litigation.

Sincerely,

Mr. Charles Drumm

Assistant County Counsel
Office of the County Counsel
County of Riverdale
15000 Civic Center Way
Dixon, Columbia

PT-A: SELECTED ANSWER 2

OFFICE OF THE COUNTY COUNSEL

County of Riverdale

1500 Civic Center Way

Dixon, Columbia

July 26, 2016

Michael Standish

Standish & Lobert LLP

1616 Oak Street

Dixon, Columbia

Re: Intended Conveyance of Wildomar Property

Dear Mr. Standish:

We represent the Riverdale Regional Park District (hereinafter "District") and Pamela Walls, the District's General Manager, in this case. We are in receipt of your letter to Ms. Walls dated July 22, 2016. We have reviewed the letter as well as your factual and legal conclusions outlined therein. Please find our position and analysis of the law correctly applied to this matter below.

Statement of District's Position

The position of District is as follows. Under the Columbia Regional Park District Act (hereinafter "Act"), real property is "actually dedicated" by a district, and thereby becomes subject to a requirement that it may validly be conveyed only with voter consent, only if the district's board of directors adopts a resolution dedicating the property. District's Board of Directors has never adopted such a resolution dedicating the Wildomar Property and therefore, District never needed to seek or obtain voter's consent for Wildomar's conveyance.

District's Position that it May Validly Convey Wildomar Without Voter-Consent is Sound Under the Facts and Law

Real Property Is "Actually Dedicated" only by Resolution by District's Board of Directors Under Section 40

District's position is plainly supported by the language of Section 40. Section 40 provides that "an easement or any other interest in real property may be actually dedicated for park purposes by the adoption of a resolution by the board of directors, and any interest so dedicated may be conveyed only as provided in this section." Moreover, this section provides that "[a] district may not validly convey any interest in real property actually dedicated and used for park purposes without the consent of a majority of the voters of the district voting at a special election called by the board and held for that purpose." A plain and common sense reading of this section provides both the prohibition on the sale of certain properties and to which properties such prohibition shall apply. The prohibition applies to those properties "actually dedicated and used for park purposes," which, as explained in the same section, are those adopted by a resolution of the board.

Here, the board never passed a resolution finding that the Wildomar Property be actually dedicated for park purposes. Indeed, as is evident in the history of the purchasing of Wildomar, it was obtained with the hopes that it could be someday used as such, but it was never dedicated for that use. Wildomar Property was held pending obtaining of the funds necessary to develop the property into a regional park but, when the funds were not able to be obtained, and it became a health and safety liability, District chose to forgo their desires with the property and sell it. This was permissible because at no time did District ever pass a resolution that actually dedicated Wildomar property to a regional park purpose. In absence of such, the provision regarding its sale was never triggered and District was free to sell and dispose of the property as they saw fit.

"Actually Dedicated" in Section 40 and "Dedicated" in Section 65 are not Identical

Your letter states that "dedicated" in Section 65 and "actually dedicated" in Section 40 are identical and, that if they were not identical, Section 65 would be rendered meaningless. However, both assumptions are incorrect.

A Plain Reading of Section 40 and Section 65 Reveals They Are Not Identical

The rules of construction provide that a court will read provisions according to their plain language. The plain language of these provisions is that one refers to property that has been "dedicated" while the other refers to property "actually dedicated." The rules of construction also suggest that the court will read the provisions in a way in which it will not render any part surplusage. To read, as you suggest, "actually dedicated" and "dedicated" as identical would be to render the word "actually" as surplusage and to dispose of a word specifically placed in the Act by the Columbia legislature as meaningless. It is clear that the word was placed in the act to differentiate between the types of dedication. To ignore the word "actually" would be to dispose of the express will of the Columbia legislature. Thus, according to a plain reading approach which the court would employ, the words used in the two sections are not actually identical.

Section 65 Has a Separate and Distinct Meaning from Section 40

Moreover, even if they were identical, Section 65 would not be meaningless. Courts have held that provisions like Section 65 create a public trust over all of the district's property, with the district itself as the owner of legal title, the residents as the owners of beneficial title, and the district's board of directors as the trustees. These provisions have been held to exempt the property from execution, levy, and sale, solely to protect the district's residents. Thus the purpose of Section 65 is entirely different from Section 40. Section 65 prohibits districts from taking such actions as selling off property to pay for judgments against them. It requires the board to act as trustees in good faith and not to use the property vested in them inappropriately. It does not prohibit the sale to benefit the public and still authorizes District to "use, acquire, manage, occupy, and possess property." Section 40, to the contrary, provides extra provisions restricting the sale of certain properties, which Section 65 does not touch on. Section 40 provides extra protection that Section 65 does not provide by requiring a public vote before any property is sold, but only as to those properties which have been "actually dedicated," meaning that the board has passed a resolution dedicating them. Therefore, it makes sense that Section 40 would require a higher showing of dedication, thus calling it "actual dedication," than does Section 65's "dedication," because Section 40 provides for a greater level of protection for the public. Thus, Section 65 is entirely meaningful even though it is separate and distinct from Section 40. It requires the board to act as trustees and in good faith and should not be convoluted as meaningless.

Adoption of Resolution by District's Board is a Method for Both Easements and "Any Other" Real Property Interest

Your letter states that the adoption of a resolution by the board is an alternative method of actual dedication for an easement under Section 40, but not for any other real property interest. However, this assertion violates the very principles of construction that courts use when reading statutes. As stated above, courts will read the provision in its plain, common sense language and will read it in a way that avoids surplusage. Again, the purpose is to conduct a reading in a way that avoids surplusage because to find surplusage would be to ignore the intent of the Columbia legislature in placing certain language or certain provisions in their statutes. It is unclear as to how Section 40 could be read to only apply to easements, excluding other real property interests. A plain reading of the statute reveals that it expressly applies to "[a]n easement or any other interest in real property." To state that this only applies to easements is to ignore the language chosen by the legislature which plainly states that it applies to easements or other interests in real property. Because easements are not a typical interest in property, the Columbia legislature likely thought it wise to specifically state that an easement was one of the included such interests in real property subject to the section, as it may be misconstrued that they were not of the type. However, the statute also explicitly applies to "any other interest in real property." Such expansive choice of words by the Columbia legislature should be given their full, intended purpose. Such language cannot be ignored by the court. To read this section in a way that only applies to easements would be to read the "any other interest in real property" portion as mere surplusage, which a court will not do under the rules of construction. Therefore, applying a plain and sensical reading, avoiding surplusage, the court will certainly find Section 40 to apply to interests in real property other than easements.

Conclusion

In sum, District's position that it may validly convey the Wildomar Property without satisfying the Act's voter-consent requirements is sound under the facts and the law. Because there was never "actual dedication," there never needed to be a public vote on the matter as Section 40 was never triggered. Accordingly, District acted lawfully.

Ms. Santa Maria's Position is Legally and Factually Unsound

Wildomar Property Was Not "Actually Dedicated"

<u>Common Law Dedication does not Apply in the Face of a Relevant Statute</u>

In your letter, you state that, first, the Wildomar Property was dedicated under common law. However, common law dedication is inapplicable here. The case to which you site, *Baldwin*, dealt only with common law dedication. Seemingly, there was no statute setting forth the standard for dedication in that city (the City of Lake Alston). However, that is not the case here. There is an applicable statute here, which is Columbia Regional Park District Act Section 40, that specifically describes when property is "actually dedicated." Because there is a statute specifically on point here, common law dedication does not apply. Common law dedication only applies in the absence of a relevant statute. (*See Osuna on Real Property*). Because there is a specific statute which sets forth the terms for dedication in Columbia, common law dedication is not available.

Even if Common Law Dedication Did Apply, Wildomar Park Was Not Dedicated

Even if, as your letter asserts, common law dedication did in fact apply, it was not established here. As you agree, common law dedication applies when there is an offer by a private owner and an acceptance by a public entity, having the character of a gift as well as a contract. In *Baldwin*, the case to which you site in support of this proposition, the court elaborated further. The court held that common law dedication entails an offer by a private owner, and acceptance by a public entity, of real property subject to a specified restricted public use in perpetuity. Your understanding of common law dedication leaves out a key aspect: that the offer and acceptance include a restriction on use in perpetuity. In *Baldwin*, for example, the court found that there was no dedication because the city did not actually accept a restriction on public use. There, the original agreement was that the public use on the conveyed property would be restricted to public recreation purposes. There was a lapse in between the offer and acceptance such to form the contract and, after a period of time, when the arrangement was revisited, no such use restriction was agreed upon in the ultimate conveyance.

There was no such use restriction agreed upon in the ultimate conveyance here either. Indeed, Ms. Potts did include such an attempted use restriction in her grant deed to District. In her deed, she stated that Wildomar be used "for park purposes in perpetuity." However, such deed came at the end of the negotiation and contract period and such deed was signed only by Ms. Potts. The agreement for the purchase of the property, which was signed by both Ms. Potts and District's representative, Ms. Patricia Smith, contained no mention of any restriction. The agreement contained a description of the property, the price at which it was to be sold, the additional value that could be obtained was provided for as a gift, and the date for closing was provided. The agreement is completely devoid of evidence that there was to be a use restriction on the land. Again, the only evidence of such use restriction was provided for in the deed, which came on the day of closing, from Ms. Potts to District. It was neither signed nor acknowledged by District nor its representatives. This restriction simply was not negotiated for; thus there was no acceptance by District of this condition. Accordingly, District cannot be said to have accepted a use restriction that it neither negotiated for nor signed in agreement with.

In sum, while the ultimate property was contracted for (offered and accepted) the use restriction was not. Accordingly, like in *Baldwin*, District then cannot be bound by common law dedication because there was no acceptance of the use restriction and thus there was no common law dedication.

A Real Property Interest Is Not Dedicated by a Regional Park Simply by Acquisition Under Section 65

Again, as stated above, your contention that real property can be dedicated simply by acquisition under Section 65 is misguided. Section 65 is separate and distinct from Section 40. Section 40 contains elevated protections and a higher level of public participation for certain lands that have been "actually dedicated" while Section 65 provides broad, general principles for the requirements of a board to act as trustees in good faith for the benefit of the citizens in terms of the property that it acquires. In order to qualify for the protections of Section 40, requiring a public vote, the property must be that which is "actually dedicated" not just "dedicated" under Section 65. The protections that Ms. Santa Maria is arguing for are those of Section 40 which requires a higher level of dedication than does Section 65. Mere acquisition under the terms of Section 65 does not entitle the public to a vote before property is sold. If the legislature had intended so, they would not have included the term "actually dedicated" under Section 40 which requires the public vote in certain circumstances.

Wildomar Property Was Not "Used" For Park Purposes

In addition, it is necessary that Wildomar Property have been used for park purposes such as to trigger the prohibition on conveyance without voter consent of Section 40. Your letter states that "actual use" is established because Wildomar Property has functioned as a regional park, although it was never developed into a regional park. This conclusion is without merit. Wildomar Property never actually functioned as a regional park. It is true that it was used by hikers, hunters, and especially birdwatchers. However, mere use by the public alone is not sufficient to state that a property is being used as a regional park. Indeed it is also true that it was never posted to keep out the public. These factors are not dispositive on the issue though. The public uses many areas, some of which are not permitted, that are not regional parks.

Chiefly, Wildomar Property was never developed into a regional park. Your letter agrees with this fact. However, it also never functioned as such despite being frequented by the aforementioned individuals. At the entrance to the property, there was a sign stating that it was the "future site" of Wildomar Park. It is clear the District was attempting to inform the public that it was not currently functioning as a park but that, hopefully, in the future, it would be open to such use. In addition, the common trademarks of regional parks were not present at Wildomar Property. There was no parking, there were no restrooms, and there were no other facilities common to regional parks. There is no evidence that District ever held Wildomar Property out to be a public park, despite that it may have tolerated or not known of trespassing occurring there. A public park is one where individuals go with the consent of the district, not one which is used by the public on their own free will without permission. It simply cannot be said that those using Wildomar Property without permission, consent, or invitation of District somehow transformed its status into that of a regional park. It was never funded nor operated at the district level as such and thus cannot be said to have been used for park purposes.

Conclusion

The arguments set forth in your letter are not appropriate under the law. Wildomar was never "actually dedicated" within the meaning of Section 40. Moreover, neither Section 65 nor the common law meaning of dedication apply here and, even if the common law meaning of dedication did so comply, Wildomar Property was not dedicated within that meaning. Therefore, there was no dedication under the law such as to trigger the voter consent requirements of Section 40.

Conclusion

In light of the foregoing, it is District's intent to proceed with the sale. It is our informed position that Ms. Santa Maria's arguments are not meritorious under the law. Accordingly, please be advised that District plans to, and will so, go forward with the conveyance not withstanding Ms. Santa Maria's threatened litigation.

Sincerely,

Charles Drumm
Assistant County Counsel

July 2016

California
Bar
Examination

Performance Test B
INSTRUCTIONS AND FILE

WONG v. PAVLIK FOODS, INC.

Instructions ....

FILE

WONG v. PAVLIK FOODS, INC.

<u>INSTRUCTIONS</u>

1. This performance test is designed to evaluate your ability to handle a select number of legal authorities in the context of a factual problem involving a client.

2. The problem is set in the fictional State of Columbia, one of the United States.

3. You will have two sets of materials with which to work: a File and a Library.

4. The File contains factual materials about your case. The first document is a memorandum containing the instructions for the tasks you are to complete.

5. The Library contains the legal authorities needed to complete the tasks. The case reports may be real, modified, or written solely for the purpose of this performance test. If the cases appear familiar to you, do not assume that they are precisely the same as you have read before. Read each thoroughly, as if it were new to you. You should assume that cases were decided in the jurisdictions and on the dates shown. In citing cases from the Library, you may use abbreviations and omit page citations.

6. You should concentrate on the materials provided, but you should also bring to bear on the problem your general knowledge of the law. What you have learned in law school and elsewhere provides the general background for analyzing the problem; the File and Library provide the specific materials with which you must work.

7. Although there are no parameters on how to apportion your time, you should allow yourself sufficient time to thoroughly review the materials and organize your planned response.

8. Your response will be graded on its compliance with instructions and on its content, thoroughness, and organization.

LAW OFFICES OF JEFFREY SU

4130 Hellman Court, Suite 104

Riverdale, Columbia

INTEROFFICE MEMORANDUM

TO: Applicant

FROM: Jeff Su

DATE: July 28, 2016

RE: Wong v. Pavlik Foods, Inc.

Our client, Arnold Wong, was until recently the head bookkeeper and payroll administrator at Pavlik Foods, Inc., a large meat processor here in Riverdale. He was fired last week and has asked us to represent him in a suit against Pavlik to recover unpaid wages. I know we can sue to recover his unpaid wages and associated civil penalties for him individually.

In the course of the interview, Mr. Wong revealed information suggesting that Pavlik has for a number of years engaged in widespread wage and hour violations with respect to its meat processing employees.

According to Mr. Wong, Pavlik averages about 400 wage earners a year working in those occupations. It strikes me that we may have an opportunity to file a significant class or representative action on behalf of all those employees, and Mr. Wong is willing to be the class representative. There are two possibilities: (1) a class action under Columbia Business Code section 17200, called the Unfair Competition Law ("UCL"), and (2) a representative action under Columbia Labor Code section 2699, known as the Private Attorney General Act ("PAGA"). Each possibility presents some legal impediments that I need your help in working through.

Please draft a memorandum explaining the following:

1. Will the facts available to us support certification of a class of current and former employees for recovery of back wages under the UCL?

2. What argument can be made that Wong can bring a representative claim under PAGA on behalf of current and former employees for *back wages* without having to satisfy class certification requirements?

3. As to what monetary relief we can obtain, the following questions remain:

   (a) Under the UCL, who may recover civil penalties?

   (b) Under PAGA, are there any prerequisites we need to satisfy before we can file suit?

   (c) Under PAGA, do the employees get to keep all the civil penalties we might recover?

In drafting your memorandum, do not include a statement of facts, but be sure to use the facts in reaching and supporting your conclusions.

TRANSCRIPT OF INTERVIEW OF ARNOLD WONG

July 25, 2016

JEFF SU: Hello, Mr. Wong – Arnold. I'm glad you could come in to see me today. You can give me the details of what we talked about briefly in our telephone conversation a few days ago. So let's start at the beginning.

ARNOLD WONG: Well, Bruce Pavlik, the boss at Pavlik Foods, fired me last week because I kept questioning him about some of the payroll practices at the company.

SU: How long had you worked for Pavlik and what was your job there?

WONG: I worked there since about November 1996 – something like that. My job was always head bookkeeper, and then in the last few years I was also the payroll administrator. You know, calculating the weekly payrolls, making up the payroll summaries, and giving them to Mr. Pavlik so he could pay the employees – actually, he'd give the payroll to the different department heads, who would actually hand out the pay to the employees.

SU: Tell me a little about Pavlik's business.

WONG: It's a meat processing plant. They get the carcasses from local suppliers – beef, lamb, and pork – and butcher it for the market. They ship all over the states – some frozen, some fresh.

SU: Okay. You told me on the phone that you wanted me to help you get some unpaid wages that Pavlik owes you, right?

WONG: Yeah. I was supposed to be paid fifteen dollars an hour. In the last year or so, work got so busy that I worked straight through my one-hour lunch period, eating lunch at my desk. When I would turn in my timesheet, Mr. Pavlik would deduct that hour and not pay me for it, telling me that I was supposed to take a lunch period and it wasn't his fault if I didn't.

SU: Is that it? Just non-payment for your lunch period?

WONG: No. I almost always worked nine or ten hours a day and most of the time, except around the year-end holidays, I worked six days a week – Sunday was my only day off. Sometimes he would give me a few dollars extra for, as he'd say, my "devotion" to work. But he never paid me for overtime like the law requires – at time and one-half.

SU: Were those the things that, when you questioned him about, he fired you for?

WONG: That was part of it. But I was also always being questioned by the plant workers about why they were being shorted. I mean, in the last couple of years I pointed out a number of things about payroll that I thought were wrong.

SU: Like what sorts of things?

WONG: Usually, he'd just tell me to do as I was told and not to make an issue of it – it was "none of my business," as he put it. But the things I questioned him about affected not just me, but almost all of the hourly plant workers. When he fired me, he told me that he was getting sick and tired of me questioning him all the time and, since I couldn't mind my own business, he told me to clean out my desk and leave. He didn't even pay me what he owed me for the last week's work.

SU: Well, first of all, how many hourly plant workers does Pavlik have?

WONG: It varies, but over a period of a year, I'd say about 350 to 400. It's hard to keep track because there's lots of turnover. My guess is that a lot of them are in the country illegally.

SU: Do you think the fact that they're illegals has anything to do with the payroll practices?

WONG: Absolutely. Mr. Pavlik can get away with a lot of stuff because the employees are afraid to complain. Anyone who does complain gets fired – that's why there's so much turnover.

SU: Okay. Tell me the kinds of payroll practices that you think were wrong at Pavlik.

WONG: There were so many things. He'd make little side deals with individual employees, so it's hard to say whether any one thing affected more than just a few of the hourly workers – maybe the carcass handlers would get one deal, the skinners another deal, the deboners yet another deal, and so forth for all the different groups in the plant. Each week Mr. Pavlik would hand me some handwritten notes telling me how to figure the pay for some of them and different notes for others.

SU: Well, were there some things that generally affected all the hourly workers?

WONG: Yeah. One thing that was fairly common was that he wouldn't give them pay stubs that explained their pay, and they were always coming to me to try to get me to explain why they were paid one amount rather than what they thought they were entitled to.

SU: What else?

WONG: I can't say there was any one thing that applied to all the workers – as I said, Mr. Pavlik was always changing the deal for different groups. For example, the minimum wage is $8.00 per hour. I know there were some workers, mostly the four- or five-person cleanup crew, who were paid less than the minimum wage. The most valuable workers were the butchers – they usually got paid overtime if they worked overtime, but nobody else did – and almost everyone worked overtime during different periods. I used to get calls from guys that Pavlik had fired wanting to know when they were going to get their final pay. He always made them wait at least a few days, and I know a lot of them never did get their final pay. Sometimes, Mr. Pavlik would pay them in cash about half of what he really owed them and make them sign a release before he'd give them the money. Time off for lunch was pretty much a hit-and-miss proposition – again, some workers got time off, others didn't. All kinds of stuff like that happened all the time.

SU: Did Pavlik keep time and pay records?

WONG: Yeah, some, but not accurate ones. I know he had a set of books he'd show government officials, but they didn't reflect the real facts. I've kept records of my own and a lot of the handwritten notes he used to hand me about how to figure the pay for different employees. I mean, it varied a lot. I know a lot of the workers also kept records of the hours they worked – they'd show them to me when they complained about not getting paid for all their hours.

SU: Did any government agency ever take action against Pavlik?

WONG: I know a few employees complained to the Labor Board, but I don't think any action was ever taken. The processing plant is way out in Gaston County, so I don't think it was on the Labor Board's priority list.

SU: Well, we'll certainly go after Pavlik for the back wages and penalties he owes you. But would you be willing to be the lead plaintiff to go after Pavlik on behalf of all the other past and present employees?

WONG: What do you mean? What's a lead plaintiff?

SU: There's something called a class action, where one person – a lead plaintiff – can sue as a representative of all the other employees affected by the same types of labor law violations. It would be a major case and would take a lot of work to put together, but I think we could do it if you'd be willing to stand up for all the rest of the workers.

WONG: Yeah, I guess so. That's what started this whole thing because I was speaking up for them. I'd like to be able to get them their money too if there's any way to do it.

SU: All right. Give me a few days to do some research, and I'll get back to you. Later, we'll have to talk about the burdens on you if you become the lead plaintiff.

WONG: Sounds good.

LAW OFFICES OF JEFFREY SU

4130 Hellman Court, Suite 104

Riverdale, Columbia

INTEROFFICE MEMORANDUM

TO: File

FROM: Jeff Su

DATE: July 25, 2016

RE: Wong v. Pavlik Foods, Inc. – Possible Violations of Columbia
             Labor Code

Based on preliminary information I obtained in my interview with Arnold Wong, I did some quick research to track the possible violations of the Columbia Labor Code at Pavlik Foods and the possible penalties that go along with the violations. Here they are:

Section 201:   Failure to pay all wages due upon discharge from employment

Section 203:   Additional wages up to 30 day's pay (waiting time penalty) for violation of Section 201

Section 206.5:   Unlawful to require release from employee as a condition to receiving wages due

Section 226:   Requirement for pay stubs showing hours, rate of pay, and wage calculation

Section 226.7:   One hour's extra pay due for each missed meal period

Section 510:   Requirement to pay time and one-half for overtime after 8 hours a day or 40 hours a week

Section 512:   Requirement for meal period of specified length during work shift

Section 1194:   Failure to pay minimum wage; liquidated damages up to twice the amount found due

Sections 210, 225.5, 558: These sections impose penalties to be assessed against the employer for violations of the foregoing sections; the penalties are between $50 and $100 per violation, per employee for the first violation, and between $100 and $200 per violation, per employee for subsequent violations.

These are all penalties for Labor Code violations. They can be recovered by the Labor Commissioner, who is the head of the Division of Labor Standards, which, in turn, is a subdivision of the Labor and Workforce Development Agency of the State of Columbia. The penalties listed above, as well as penalties specifically provided for in PAGA, are all recoverable under PAGA.

In addition, the UCL provides for a civil penalty of $2,500 per violation, but I'm not sure how that works or who can recover it.

Hard to say, at this early stage, what the aggregate back wages and penalties could be, but certainly in the millions if Wong's information pans out

July 2016

California
Bar
Examination

Performance Test B
LIBRARY

WONG v. PAVLIK FOODS, INC.

LIBRARY

EXCERPTS FROM THE COLUMBIA BUSINESS CODE
(Unfair Competition Law)

Section 17200.   As used in this chapter, unfair competition shall mean and include any unlawful, unfair or fraudulent business act or practice.

Section 17203.   The court may make such orders or judgments as may be necessary to restore to any person in interest any money or property, real or personal, which may have been acquired by means of such unfair competition. Any person may pursue representative claims or relief on behalf of others only if the claimant meets the standing requirements of Section 17204 and complies with Section 382 of the Code of Procedure.

Section 17204.   Actions for relief pursuant to this chapter shall be prosecuted exclusively in a court of competent jurisdiction by the Attorney General or a district attorney or by a county counsel or by a person who has suffered injury in fact and has lost money or property as a result of the unfair competition.

Section 17206.   Any person who engages, has engaged, or proposes to engage in unfair competition shall be liable for a civil penalty not to exceed two thousand five hundred dollars ($2,500) for each violation, which shall be assessed and recovered in a civil action brought in the name of the people of the State of Columbia by the Attorney General.

EXCERPT FROM THE COLUMBIA CODE OF PROCEDURE
(Class Actions)

Section 382.   When the question is one of a common or general interest, of many persons, or when the parties are numerous, and it is impracticable to bring them all before the court, one or more may sue or defend for the benefit of all.

EXCERPT FROM THE COLUMBIA LABOR CODE

Section 558.

(a) Any employer or other person acting on behalf of an employer who violates, or causes to be violated, a section of this chapter or any provision regulating hours and days of work in this code shall be subject to a civil penalty as follows:

    (1) For any initial violation, fifty dollars ($50) for each underpaid employee for each pay period for which the employee was underpaid in addition to an amount sufficient to recover underpaid wages.

    (2) For each subsequent violation, one hundred dollars ($100) for each underpaid employee for each pay period for which the employee was underpaid in addition to an amount sufficient to recover underpaid wages.

    (3) Wages recovered pursuant to this section shall be paid to the affected employee.

(b) If upon inspection or investigation the Labor Commissioner determines that a person had paid or caused to be paid a wage for overtime work in violation of any provision of this chapter, or any provision regulating hours and days of work in this code, the Labor Commissioner may issue a citation and obtain and enforce a judgment to recover the unpaid wages.

(c) The civil penalties provided for in this section are in addition to any other civil or criminal penalty provided by law.

PRIVATE ATTORNEY GENERAL ACT
(Columbia Labor Code)

Section 2699.

(a) Notwithstanding any other provision of law, any provision of this code that provides for a civil penalty to be assessed and collected by the Labor and Workforce Development Agency or any of its departments, divisions, commissions, boards, agencies, or employees, for a violation of the Labor Code, may, as an alternative, be recovered through a civil action brought by an aggrieved employee on behalf of himself or herself and other current or former employees pursuant to the procedures specified in Section 2699.3.

(b) For purposes of this part, "aggrieved employee" means any person who was employed by the alleged violator and against whom one or more of the alleged violations was committed.

(c) For all provisions of this code except those for which a civil penalty is specifically provided, the civil penalty for a violation of these provisions is one hundred dollars ($100) for each aggrieved employee per pay period for the initial violation and two hundred dollars ($200) for each aggrieved employee per pay period for each subsequent violation.

(d) An aggrieved employee may recover the civil penalty described in subdivision (c) in a civil action pursuant to the procedures specified in Section 2699.3 filed on behalf of himself or herself and other current or former employees against whom one or more of the alleged violations was committed. Any employee who prevails in any action shall be entitled to an award of reasonable attorney's fees and costs. Nothing in this part shall operate to limit an employee's right to pursue or recover other remedies available under state or federal law, either separately or concurrently with an action taken under this part.

(e)   Civil penalties recovered by aggrieved employees shall be distributed as follows: 75 percent to the Labor and Workforce Development Agency for enforcement of labor laws and 25 percent to the aggrieved employees.

Section 2699.3.

(a)   A civil action by an aggrieved employee pursuant to Section 2699 alleging a violation of any applicable provision of the Labor Code shall commence only after the following requirements have been met:

(1)   The aggrieved employee or representative shall give written notice by certified mail to the Labor and Workforce Development Agency and the employer of the specific provisions of this code alleged to have been violated, including the facts and theories to support the alleged violation.

(2)   The agency shall notify the employer and the aggrieved employee or representative by certified mail that it does not intend to investigate the alleged violation within 30 calendar days of the postmark date of the notice received pursuant to paragraph (1). Upon receipt of that notice or if no notice is provided within 33 calendar days of the postmark date of the notice given pursuant to paragraph (1), the aggrieved employee may commence a civil action pursuant to Section 2699.

ARENTZ v. ANGELINA DAIRY, INC.
Columbia Supreme Court (2009)

The sole issue in this case is whether an employee who, on behalf of himself and other employees, sues an employer under the Unfair Competition Law (Business Code Section 17200, et seq.) for Labor Code violations must satisfy class action certification requirements, but that those requirements need not be met when an employee's representative action against an employer is seeking civil penalties under the Private Attorney General Act of 2004 (Labor Code Section 2699).

Jose A. Arentz sued his former employer, Angelina Dairy. In the first cause of action in the First Amended Complaint, Plaintiff alleged violations of the Labor Code *on behalf of himself as well as other current and former employees of Defendant.* The claim is that Defendant had violated the Labor Code by failing to pay all wages due, to provide itemized wage statements, to maintain adequate payroll records, to pay all wages due upon termination, to provide rest and meal periods, to offset proper amounts for employer-provided housing, and to provide necessary tools and equipment. In this cause of action, Plaintiff sought to recover under the Private Attorney General Act all statutory penalties associated with the Labor Code violations.

The second cause of action alleged violations of the Unfair Competition Law *on behalf of himself as well as other current and former employees of Defendant* based on Defendant's failures to credit Plaintiff for all hours worked, to pay overtime wages, to pay wages when due, to pay wages due upon termination, to provide rest and meal periods, and to obtain written authorization for deducting or offsetting wages.

The trial court granted Defendant's motion to strike the second cause of action on the ground that Plaintiff failed to comply with the pleading requirements for class actions. Plaintiff petitioned the Court of Appeal for a writ of mandate. That court held that the causes of action brought in a representative capacity alleging violations of the Unfair Competition Law, but not the representative claims under the Labor Code's Private Attorney General Act of 2004, were subject to class action certification requirements. We granted Plaintiff's petition for review.

Plaintiff contends the Court of Appeal erred in holding that to bring representative claims (that is, claims on behalf of others as well as himself) under the Unfair Competition Law, he must comply with class action requirements. We disagree.

In a class action, the plaintiff, in a representative capacity, seeks recovery on behalf of other persons. A party seeking certification of a class bears the burden of establishing that there is an ascertainable class and a well-defined community of interest among the class members. If the trial court grants certification, class members are notified that any class member may opt out of the class and that the judgment will bind all members who do not opt out. A class action cannot be settled or dismissed without court approval.

The Unfair Competition Law prohibits "any unlawful, unfair or fraudulent business act or practice." It provides that a private plaintiff may bring a representative action under this law only if the plaintiff has "suffered injury in fact and has lost money or property as a result of such unfair competition" and "complies with Section 382 of the Code of Procedure, which provides that "when the question is one of a common or general interest, of many persons, or when the parties are numerous, and it is impracticable to bring them all before the court, one or more may sue or defend for the benefit of all." This court has interpreted Section 382 of the Code of Procedure as authorizing class actions. The Unfair Competition Law also provides that *"Any person may pursue representative claims or relief on behalf of others only if the claimant meets the standing requirements of Section 17204 and complies with Section 382 of the Code of Procedure."* Read together, these provisions leave no doubt that a plaintiff seeking to maintain a class action under the Unfair Competition Law must satisfy the stringent requirements for showing community of interest among the represented parties, common issues of law and fact, adequate representation of the class interests by the nominal parties, and sufficient numerosity.

We turn now to the next issue – whether class action certification requirements must also be satisfied when an aggrieved employee seeks civil penalties for himself and other employees under the Labor Code's Private Attorney General Act of 2004 for an employer's alleged Labor Code violations.

In September 2003, the Legislature enacted the Private Attorney General Act of 2004 (Labor Code Section 2698, et seq.). The Legislature declared that adequate financing of labor law enforcement was necessary to achieve maximum compliance with state labor laws, that staffing levels for labor law enforcement agencies had declined and were unlikely to keep pace with the future growth of the labor market, and that it was therefore in the public interest to allow aggrieved employees, acting as private attorneys general, to recover civil penalties for Labor Code violations, with the understanding that labor law enforcement agencies were to retain primacy over private enforcement efforts.

Under this legislation, an "aggrieved employee" may bring a civil action personally and on behalf of other current or former employees to recover civil penalties for Labor Code violations. Of the civil penalties recovered, 75 percent goes to the Labor and Workforce Development Agency, leaving the remaining 25 percent for the "aggrieved employees."

Before bringing a civil action for statutory penalties, an employee must comply with Labor Code Section 2699.3, requiring the employee to give written notice of the alleged Labor Code violations to both the employer and the Labor and Workforce Development Agency, and the notice must describe facts and theories supporting the violation. If the agency notifies the employee and the employer that it does not intend to investigate (as occurred here), or if the agency fails to respond within 33 days, the employee may then bring a civil action against the employer.

Here, Plaintiff's first cause of action seeks civil penalties under the Private Attorney General Act of 2004 for himself and other employees of Defendant for alleged violations of various Labor Code provisions. Defendant challenges the Court of Appeal's holding here that to bring this cause of action, Plaintiff need *not* satisfy class action certification requirements.

The court relied on these three reasons: (1) Labor Code Section 2699, subdivision (a), states that "[n]otwithstanding any other provision of law" an aggrieved employee may bring an action against the employer "on behalf of himself or herself and other current or former employees"; (2) unlike the Unfair Competition Law's Section 17203, the Private Attorney General Act of 2004 does not expressly require that representative actions comply with Code of Procedure Section 382; and (3) a private plaintiff suing under this act is essentially bringing a law enforcement action designed to protect the public.

At issue here is whether such actions *must* be brought as a class action subject to the traditional class certification requirements.

Defendant urges us to construe the Private Attorney General Act of 2004 as requiring that all actions under that act be brought as traditional class actions. We decline.

An employee plaintiff suing, as here, under the Private Attorney General Act of 2004, does so as the proxy or agent of the state's labor law enforcement agencies. The Act's declared purpose is to supplement enforcement actions by public agencies, which lack adequate resources to bring all such actions themselves. In a lawsuit brought under the Act, the employee plaintiff represents the same legal right and interest as state labor law enforcement agencies –

namely, recovery of civil penalties that otherwise would have been assessed and collected by the Labor Workforce Development Agency. The employee plaintiff may bring the action only after giving written notice to both the employer and the Labor and Workforce Development Agency and 75 percent of any civil penalties recovered must be distributed to the Labor and Workforce Development Agency. Because collateral estoppel applies not only against a party to the prior action in which the issue was determined, but also against those for whom the party acted as an agent or proxy, a judgment in an employee's action under the Act binds not only that employee but also the state labor law enforcement agencies.

Because an aggrieved employee's action under the Private Attorney General Act of 2004 functions as a substitute for an action brought by the government itself, a judgment in that action binds all those, including nonparty aggrieved employees, who would be bound by a judgment in an action brought by the government. The Act authorizes a representative action only for the purpose of seeking statutory penalties for Labor Code violations, and an action to recover civil penalties is fundamentally a law enforcement action designed to protect the public and not to benefit private parties. When a government agency is authorized to bring an action on behalf of an individual or in the public interest, and a private person lacks an independent legal right to bring the action, a person who is not a party but who is represented by the agency is bound by the judgment as though the person were a party. Accordingly, with respect to the recovery of civil penalties, nonparty employees as well as the government are bound by the judgment in an action brought under the Act.

As Defendant points out, there remain situations in which nonparty aggrieved employees may profit from a judgment in an action brought under the Private Attorney General Act of 2004. This is why: Recovery of civil penalties under the act requires proof of a Labor Code violation, and for some Labor Code violations there are remedies in addition to civil penalties (for example, lost wages and work benefits, unpaid overtime compensation, one hour of additional pay for missed meal periods, etc.). Therefore, if an employee plaintiff prevails in an action under the Act for civil penalties by proving that the employer has committed a Labor Code violation, the defendant employer will be bound by the resulting judgment. Nonparty employees may then, by invoking collateral estoppel, use the judgment against the employer to obtain remedies other than civil penalties for the same Labor Code violations. If the employer had prevailed, however, the nonparty employees, because they were not given notice of the action or afforded any opportunity to be heard, would not be bound by the judgment as to remedies other than civil penalties.

The potential for nonparty aggrieved employees to benefit from a favorable judgment under the act without being bound by an adverse judgment, however, is not unique to the Private Attorney General Act of 2004. It also exists when an action seeking civil penalties for Labor Code violations is brought by a government agency rather than by an aggrieved employee suing under the Private Attorney General Act of 2004, because an action under the Act is designed to protect the public, and the potential impact on remedies other than civil penalties is ancillary to the action's primary objective.

The judgment of the Court of Appeal is affirmed.

SUPERIOR COURT IN AND FOR THE COUNTY OF BELDEN
STATE OF COLUMBIA

ABEL WESTLUND, individually and on behalf of all others similarly situated, Plaintiffs, vs. PALLADIN FARMS, INC., Defendant.	Case No. CIV-39-14430-01 <u>DECISION DENYING CLASS CERTIFICATION</u>

Plaintiff, Abel Westlund, a field foreman previously employed by defendant Palladin Farms, Inc., a row crop producer and packer in Belden County, brought this action to recover unpaid wages for himself and a class of employees described as consisting of "field and packing house workers employed by Palladin Farms during the 1999 and 2000 spring harvests." Alleging numerous violations of the Columbia Labor Code, Plaintiff bases his claim for recovery upon Columbia Business Code Section 17200, et seq.

After conducting discovery on the composition of the class, Plaintiff moved for certification of the described class and for an order allowing him to maintain the action as a class action on behalf of all current and former employees in the class. In the relevant period – the 1999 and 2000 spring harvests – there were approximately 150 field workers and 75 packing house workers, some employed for the entirety of each of the harvests and others for varying periods of time. Defendant opposed the motion for certification on the general ground that Plaintiff has failed to show that a class action is appropriate.

The complaint alleges that Defendant employed him, the field workers, and the packing house workers in violation of various sections of the Labor Code. For purposes of this motion, the court takes the allegations as being true. Plaintiff asserts that he was the only salaried employee in the proposed class and that Defendant unlawfully withheld portions of his weekly salary purportedly to cover expenses for rental and meals furnished to him.

The claim he asserts on behalf of the field workers is that Defendant routinely short-counted the piecework chits submitted by the fieldworkers, thus depriving them of payments for varying amounts of crops picked and turned in. The claims asserted on behalf of the packing house workers are that some of them were paid less than the minimum wage and that some of them were not paid for time spent at the beginning of each shift for assembling and otherwise preparing crates for the packing process and at the end of each shift cleaning up their work areas.

Defendant, in opposition to the motion for class certification, properly points out that the alleged pay practices involve a wide range of Labor Code sections and affect different employees in different ways, such that the claims are not susceptible of resolution on a class basis, i.e., that there are insufficient questions of law and fact common to the proposed class members.

DISCUSSION

Class actions in this state are authorized under Section 382 of the Columbia Code of Procedure. Our Supreme Court has held that this code section is to be applied and interpreted in the same way as Rule 23 of the Federal Rules of Civil Procedure is applied to class actions brought in the federal courts. See, *Campbell v. Omnibus Industries, Inc.* (Colum. Supreme Ct. 1999).

Rule 23 prescribes the following basic essentials for maintenance of class actions:

(1) Numerosity: The class is so numerous that joinder of all members is impracticable;

(2) Commonality: There are questions of law or fact common to the class;

(3) Typicality: The claims or defenses of the representative parties are typical of the claims or defenses of the class; and

(4) Adequacy of Representation: The representative parties will fairly and adequately protect the interests of the class.

The number of potential class members satisfies the numerosity requirement, but the court finds that Plaintiff has failed to establish the remaining requirements for maintenance of this action as a class action. The kinds of wage violations alleged vary from group to group within the proposed class and the factual components necessary to establish the violations are likely to vary from individual to individual. The claim of plaintiff, Westlund, is not at all typical of the types of claims he asserts on behalf of the other members of the proposed class, and, because of those differences, it is not at all clear that Plaintiff will be able to fairly and adequately represent the diverse interests of the proposed class members.

Thus, the court is unable to find that questions of fact and law *common to class members* predominates over questions of fact and law affecting only *individual members*.

For that reason, Plaintiff's motion for class certification is denied.

Date: March 30, 2001

/s/ Alfred P. Simms

Alfred P. Simms

Judge of the Superior Court

TALBOTT v. EUPHONIC SYNTHESIZERS, LLC
Columbia Court of Appeal (2010)

In 2009, plaintiff, Lance Talbott, on behalf of himself and a class of employees, sued his employer Euphonic Synthesizers, LLC for wages unlawfully withheld in violation of the Columbia Labor Code. Plaintiff alleged two causes of action: one for restitution to the class under Columbia Business Code Section 17200, the Unfair Competition Law (UCL), and the other a representative claim under Columbia Labor Code Section 2699, the Private Attorney General Act (PAGA). In each, he sought to recover unpaid wages and statutory penalties.

Plaintiff moved the trial court to allow him to conduct discovery on the class issues relating to the Section 17200 claim, i.e., the names, addresses, job classifications, and wage records of current employees and former employees during the period of the applicable statute of limitations. The court denied the motion and, in addition, ruled that the suit could not be maintained as a class action, for the reason that the wage claims on behalf of the class appeared to lack merit. The trial court also dismissed Plaintiff's PAGA claim for the recovery of unpaid wages on behalf of the class.

We believe the trial court abused its discretion in denying Plaintiff's motion for discovery on the class issues. Whether the class claims lack merit is a question of fact based on the proof that Plaintiff might be able to bring to bear once the identity and circumstances of the class members are determined. Plaintiff should at least have the opportunity to produce the evidence, at which time the question of the merits can be tested.

Plaintiff urges this court also to reverse the trial court's dismissal of his representative PAGA claim for unpaid wages.

The seminal case is *Arentz v. Angelina Dairy, Inc.* (Colum. Supreme Ct. 2009). The Court held there that a plaintiff may maintain a representative action under PAGA to recover civil penalties without having to satisfy the traditional requirements for certification of a class. In response to the defendant's assertion that to allow such a representative action without the safeguards of a class action certification has adverse due process and collateral estoppel consequences upon the unnamed class members, the Court stated:

> Because an aggrieved employee's action under the Private Attorney General Act of 2004 functions as a substitute for an action brought by the government itself, a judgment in that action binds all those, including nonparty aggrieved employees, who would be bound by a judgment in an action brought by the government. The Act authorizes a representative action *only for the purpose of seeking statutory penalties for Labor Code violations*, and an action to recover civil penalties is fundamentally a law enforcement action designed to protect the public and not to benefit private parties.

Defendant, Euphonic Synthesizers, asserted in the court below that the italicized language foreclosed any claim that Plaintiff could assert for anything other than civil penalties, i.e., unpaid wages are not penalties, so, claims Defendant, they cannot be a component of any PAGA recovery.

Plaintiff, on the other hand, cites to Labor Code Section 2699 (d), a subsection of PAGA, which states, "Nothing in this part shall operate to limit an employee's right to pursue or recover other remedies available under state or federal law, either separately or concurrently with an action taken under this part." Claims for recovery of unpaid wages, argues Plaintiff, are "other remedies" under the Labor Code and, therefore, can be sought "concurrently with an action taken under [PAGA]." Moreover, Plaintiff cites Labor Code Section 558, which allows the

Labor Commissioner, who is the head of the Division of Labor Standards, to issue citations for recovery of *both* unpaid wages and civil penalties.

Plaintiff also argues that the Legislature's intent in enacting PAGA was to confer upon private parties the power theretofore reserved to state labor law enforcement agencies to bring representative actions to enforce Columbia's wage and hour laws. Thus, argues Plaintiff, the logical conclusion to be drawn from the combination of Section 2699 (d) and Section 558 is that PAGA provides private individuals, standing in the shoes of the state labor law enforcement agencies, the representative action mechanism to recover unpaid wages through private enforcement of Section 558.

We believe the trial court misapprehended this question of first impression: whether one who brings a representative suit for civil penalties under PAGA can also maintain, in the same action, claims for unpaid wages for members of the class he purports to represent.

Accordingly, we reverse and remand with instructions to the trial court to allow Plaintiff to conduct reasonable discovery on the class issues. At that time, the trial court can reconsider its dismissal of Plaintiff's PAGA claim for recovery of unpaid wages in light of the foregoing observations.

PT-B: SELECTED ANSWER 1

TO: Jeff Su
FROM: Applicant
DATE: July 28, 2016
RE: Wong v. Pavlik Foods, Inc.

INTRODUCTION

You have asked me to research the legal impediments related to Arnold Wong's ("Wong") information of wage violations at Pavlik Foods, Inc. ("Pavlik" or "P"). The legal impediments related to the following two possible suits: (1) a class action under Columbia Business Code section 17200, called the Unfair Competition Law ("UCL"); and (2) a representative action under Columbia Labor Code section 2699, known as the Private Attorney General Act ("PAGA"). Under the UCL, I have determined that there are sufficient facts available to support class certification of current and former employees for recovery of back wages under the UCL. Under the PAGA, I have determined that the court will likely permit Wong to bring a representative claim under PAGA on behalf of current and former employees for back wages without having to satisfy class certification requirements. A more detailed analysis of my conclusions, along with a discussion about the monetary relief available, is below.

UCL AND PAGA REQUIREMENTS

UCL Class Certification

You have asked me to determine whether the facts at hand support certification of current and former workers under the UCL. The UCL prohibits "any unlawful, unfair or fraudulent business act or practice." <u>UCL § 17200</u>. It provides that a private plaintiff may bring a representative action under the UCL so long as the plaintiff can, she/he has proper standing and complies with class certification requirements. Therefore, Wong must have sufficient standing and meet the class certification requirements in order to bring a UCL claim.

Standing

The issue is whether Wong has sufficient standing under the UCL. To have standing under the UCL, a plaintiff (P) must show that he has "suffered injury in fact and has lost money or property as a result of such unfair competition." UCL § 17204. Here, Wong hopes to bring a UCL claim for lost wages. Per your discussion with Wong, he has suffered various injuries in fact, including (1) a week of lost wages upon discharge from employment; (2) lost wages related to the requirement to pay time and one-half for overtime after 8 hours a day or 40 hours a week; (3) lost pay for each missed meal period; and (4) lost meal period during his work shifts at Pavlik. Along with these injuries, Wong lost money as a result of Pavlik's unfair and unlawful work practices. Therefore, Wong will meet the standing requirement of injury in fact and lost money under the UCL.

Class Certification

The next issue is whether Wong can show sufficient facts to meet class certification requirements. The UCL requires that a plaintiff must comply "with Section 382 of the Code of Procedure, which provides that 'when the question is one of a common or general interest, of many persons, or when the parties are numerous, and it is impracticable to bring them all before the court, one or more may sue or defend for the benefit of all.'" The Columbia Supreme Court has interpreted Section 382 of the Code of Procedure as authorizing class actions. *Arentz v. Angelina Dairy, Inc*; See *Westlund v. Palladin Farms, Inc*. Therefore, in order for a plaintiff to maintain a class action under the UCL, the plaintiff "must satisfy the stringent requirements for showing community of interest among the represented parties, common issues of law and fact, adequate representation of the class interests by the nominal parties, and sufficient numerosity." *Arentz*; See *Westlund*. "A party seeking certification of a class bears the burden of establishing that there is an ascertainable class and a well-defined community of interest among the class members." *Arentz*. Whether class certification claims lack merit "is a question of fact based on proof that Plaintiff might be able to bring to bear once the identity and circumstances of the class members are determined." *Talbott v. Euphonic Synthesizers, LLC*. Plaintiff has the opportunity to conduct discovery on class issues in order to produce evidence of class certification. *Id.* Therefore, Wong may establish class certification requirements through discovery, but he must be able to establish (1) numerosity; (2) commonality; (3) typicality; and (4) adequacy of representation.

Numerosity

Numerosity requires a showing that "[t]he class is so numerous that joinder of all members is impracticable." *Westlund*. The superior court has found that in the span of one year, a class of 225 was a sufficient number to satisfy the numerosity requirement *Id.* (finding that 150 field workers and 75 packing house workers employed at various times and intervals during a one-year period was a sufficient number of potential class members to satisfy the numerosity requirement). Here, Wong has suggested that over a period of a year, Pavlik has about 350 to 400 hourly plant workers at varying times. Wong noted that there is a lot of turnover; however, as the court recognized in *Westlund*, over 225 workers during a year period working at various intervals is sufficient to meet numerosity. Therefore, the court will likely find Wong meets the numerosity requirement.

Commonality

Commonality requires a showing that "[t]here are questions of law or fact common to the class." *Westlund*. Specifically the questions of fact and law common to class members must "predominate[] over questions of fact and law affecting only individual members." In *Westlund*, the workers alleged wage violations that differed from group to group within the proposed class. Some class members were paid less than minimum wage, some members were not paid for time spent on the beginning and end of each shift, and other members were short-counted on payments for labor done. However, the members could not point to common wage violations that affected most or all members. As such, the court determined that the workers did not have questions of law or fact in common and could not meet the commonality requirement.

Here, Wong has described a number of wage violations that differ between workers. Wong has stated that there is not one thing that applied to all the workers because Pavlik "was always changing the deal for different groups." However, Wong did suggest that certain violations were "fairly common" to the workers. First, Wong stated that Pavlik generally failed to give the hourly workers pay stubs that explained their pay. Under Section 226, employers are required to provide pay stubs showing hours, rate of pay, and wage calculation. Wong's statements reflect that this practice was common among most workers; therefore, it provides a common question of fact or law.

Second, Wong also stated that, aside from the butchers, no other workers were paid overtime. Section 510 requires that employers pay time and one-half for overtime after 8 hours a day or 40 hours a week. Depending on how many workers are butchers, this overtime violation is also a common question of fact. Wong has suggested that butchers were the most valuable workers, so it is likely that Pavlik may have attempted to minimize the amount of workers who were butchers in order to cut costs. In any case, more discovery is necessary to truly determine how many workers were non-butchers and failed to receive overtime pay. It is likely this will satisfy as a common question.

Third, Wong suggested that many workers called him complaining about the lack of final pay checks after being fired. Section 201 requires employers to pay all wages due upon discharge from employment. Pavlik failed to do so. Provided that discovery establishes a large number of workers had this problem, this would also be a common question of fact or law.

Fourth, Wong also mentioned that Pavlik did not regularly give workers time off for lunch. Section 512 requires that employer give a meal period of specified length during a work shift, and section 226.7 requires a one hour's extra pay due for each missed meal period. Wong suggested that some workers got time off, others did not. Depending on the number of workers who did not get time off, this may be a common question of fact or law. However, based on Pavlik's treatment of Wong when he worked during lunch, it is likely that this problem was common to many workers. More discovery will help establish this commonality.

Wong also mentioned that a few workers were paid less than minimum wage, but this pertained to only four or five of the cleanup crew. This is likely not a common question of fact or law, so the court likely won't recognize it as sufficient for commonality.

Through more discovery, we may be able to obtain more certain numbers; however, the current evidence suggests that certain violations were common among most workers. Therefore, there are likely common questions of fact or law. These facts outweigh any individual violations pertaining to the few workers who did not obtain minimum wage, so a court will likely find commonality is met.

Typicality

Typicality requires that "[t]he claims or defenses of the representative parties are typical of claims or defenses of the class." *Westlund*. In *Westlund*, the plaintiff representative asserted that he was the only salaried employee in the class and that the defendant unlawfully withheld portions of his weekly salary. However, none of the class members asserted a similar claim. Therefore, the court found the representative was not typical of the members.

Here, as discussed above, there are arguably four common claims of the class, including (1) failure to give pay stubs showing hours, rate of pay, and wage calculation; (2) failure to pay time and one-half for overtime; (3) failure to pay all wages due upon discharge; and (4) failure to give a meal period or pay extra pay for missed meal periods. As a representative of the class claims, Wong must assert typical claims. Wong has asserted that he has at least three of the four common claims against Pavlik, including (1) failure to pay time and one-half for overtime; (2) failure to pay all wages due upon discharge; and (3) failure to give a meal period or pay extra pay for missed meal periods. The court may find that since Wong was a bookkeeper and payroll administrator, he was not a typical worker in Pavlik. However, unlike the plaintiff representative in _Westlund_, Wong has suffered the same claims that many worker class members suffered. Therefore, his claims are typical of the class claims, and he has met the typicality requirements.

Adequacy of Representation

Adequacy of representation requires that "[t]he representative parties fairly and adequately protect the interests of the class." _Westlund_. In _Westlund_, the court found that because of the major differences in claims between the representative salaried employee and class workers, the salaried representative was not an adequate representative. Here, however, Wong's claims against Pavlik are three of the four claims that class members have suffered against Pavlik. He has been working for Pavlik for 20 years and has access to the books and various notes from Pavlik regarding payment to workers. Because of this access, Wong can fix any inconsistencies regarding the varying payments to workers that are bound to appear in discovery. Because of his position and the claims he has asserted, Wong is an adequate representative who can protect the members' interests. Therefore, the court will find the adequacy of representation is sufficient.

Conclusion

As discussed above, it is likely that after discovery, we will have sufficient evidence to establish class certification with Wong as the representative. Wong meets the requirements of (1) numerosity, (2) commonality, (3) typicality, and (4) adequacy of representation. Therefore, the court will likely grant certification.

PAGA Claim Without Certification

You have asked me to determine whether Wong may bring a representative claim under PAGA on behalf of current and former employees for back wages without having to satisfy class certification requirements. PAGA states that an aggrieved employee may bring an action against the employer "on behalf of himself or herself and other current or former employees." PAGA §2669; *Arentz*. Courts have recognized that unlike the UCL, PAGA does not expressly require that representative actions comply with Section 382's class certification requirements. *Arentz*. An aggrieved employee suing under PAGA "does so as the proxy or agent of the state's labor law enforcement agencies." *Id*. PAGA's purpose is "to supplement enforcement actions by public agencies, which lack adequate resources to bring all such actions themselves." Id. Therefore, an employee plaintiff may act as a government agency and bring a PAGA claim on behalf of workers without class certification. *Id.* The plaintiff need only give written notice to both the employer and the Labor and Workforce Development Agency (the "Agency") and 75 percent of any civil penalties recovered must be distributed to the Agency. *Id.*; PAGA. Here, so long as Wong satisfies the definition of an "aggrieved employee," he may bring a representative claim under PAGA against Pavlik without certifying the class.

Aggrieved Employee

Under PAGA, an aggrieved employee "means any person who was employed by the alleged violator and against whom one or more of the alleged violations was committed." PAGA §2669. As discussed above, Wong has been employed by Pavlik for 20 years and suffered at least three of the alleged violations committed against the workers. Therefore, he meets the requirements of an aggrieved employee. Wong may bring a claim under PAGA on behalf of the current and former workers without certifying the class.

Recovery of Back Wages

Although PAGA allows for the recovery of civil penalties without class certification, unpaid wages (such as back wages) are not civil penalties. Therefore, the issue is whether PAGA also allows for the recovery of back wages along with the civil penalties involved. In _Talbott_, the defendant employer argued that the court in _Arentz_ foreclosed any claim that a plaintiff employee could assert without class certification for anything other than civil penalties. _Talbott_ quoting _Arentz_ ("The Act authorizes a representative action only for the purpose of seeking statutory penalties for Labor Code violations, and an action to recover civil penalties is fundamentally a law enforcement action designed to protect the public and not to benefit private parties."). However, the court in Talbott rejected the trial court's decision that representative actions in PAGA without class certification are limited to civil penalties. The court determined that PAGA specifically states that "[n]othing in this part shall operate to limit an employee's right to pursue or recover other remedies available under state or federal law, either separately or concurrently with an action taken under this part." _Talbott_; PAGA §2699. The plaintiff in _Talbott_ argued that claims for recovery of unpaid wages are "other remedies" recognized under the Labor Code. Therefore, they can be recovered "concurrently with an action taken under" PAGA. The legislature enacted PAGA in order "to confer upon private parties the power theretofore reserved to state labor law enforcement agencies to bring representative actions to enforce Columbia's wage and hour laws." _Talbott_; see _Arentz_. Section 558 of the Labor Code specifically provides the Labor Commissioner-the head of a state labor law enforcement agency-with the distinct authority to issue citations for the recovery of both unpaid wages and civil penalties. Because courts have recognized PAGA's intent to confer upon private parties the authority to enforce labor laws related to government agencies, an aggrieved employee can file claims under PAGA without class certification to recover unpaid wages through private enforcement of Section 558.

The court in _Talbott_ recognized the above arguments and noted that the lower court "misapprehended" the questions of whether an aggrieved employee who brings a representative suit for civil penalties under PAGA can also maintain, in the same action, claims for unpaid wages. _Talbott_. Although the law has not been completely settled regarding this issue, it is likely we may bring a valid claim that PAGA intended for representatives to recover both unpaid wages and civil penalties.

REMEDIES

UCL Remedies Available

The next issue is who may recover civil penalties under the UCL. In Section 17206 of UCL, "[a]ny person who engages . . . in unfair competition shall be liable for a civil penalty not to exceed two thousand five hundred dollars ($2,500) for each violation, which shall be assessed and recovered in a civil action brought in the name of the people of the State of Columbia by the Attorney General." Based on the language in the UCL, it is likely that civil penalties must be brought by the Attorney General and must be recovered in the name of the people of the State of Columbia by the Attorney General. Although PAGA allows for civil penalties to be recovered by a plaintiff employee, UCL provides no such provision. Without such a provision, it is likely that only an action by the Attorney General may recover civil penalties for the State. The class will be limited to recovering based on the statutory violations described above.

PAGA Remedies Available

Prerequisites Before Suit

As discussed above, an employee plaintiff may bring a representative claim against an employer for labor violations so long as (1) the employee representative meets the definition of an aggrieved employee; and (2) gives written notice by certified mail to both the employer and the Agency regarding the specific provisions of PAGA alleged to have been violated, including the facts and theories to support the alleged violation. PAGA §2699.3. If the Agency provides notice that it does not intend to investigate violations, or if 33 calendar days have passed since the written notice was given, the aggrieved employee may then file suit. *Id.*

As discussed above, Wong meets the aggrieved employee definition. In regards to the written notice requirement, Wong has stated that a few employees complained to the Agency, but he was not sure if any action was ever taken. According to Wong, the action may not be high on the Agency's priority list. Based on the evidence at hand, there is no evidence to suggest that the employees provided a written notice by certified mail to the Agency alleging the specific violations. Furthermore, no evidence suggests the employees gave Pavlik written notice of the violations. Therefore, before Wong may bring a representative claim under PAGA, he must first comply with the notice requirement to determine if the Agency will take any action.

Employees' Share of Civil Penalties Recovered

Assuming Wong meets the notice requirements for the PAGA claim and obtains civil penalties, PAGA requires that 75 percent of any civil penalties recovered by aggrieved employees must be distributed to the Agency for enforcement of labor law, and 25 percent will be distributed to the aggrieved employees. PAGA §2699. This requirement reflects the fact that PAGA claims brought by a representative claim of an aggrieved employee supplement enforcement actions by public agencies. Therefore, 75% of the civil penalties obtained by the aggrieved employee must be distributed to the public agency.

CONCLUSION

In conclusion, it is likely that the facts available to us support certification of a class of current and former Pavlik employees for recovery of back wages under the UCL. Furthermore, although the law is unsettled, there is a strong argument to be made that the legislature intended PAGA to allow aggrieved employees to bring a representative claim for back wages without having to satisfy class certification requirements. Finally, the monetary relief may be subject to limitations and prerequisites as discussed in depth above; however, the class will still recover a potentially substantial amount related to Pavlik's excessive Labor Code violations that have occurred during Wong's 20 years of employment.

Interoffice Memorandum

To: Jeff Su
From: Applicant
Date: July 29, 2016
Re: Wong v. Pavlik Foods, Inc.

UNFAIR COMPETITION LAW [COLUMBIA BUSINESS CODE SECTION 17200]

The first issue is whether the facts available to us support certification of a class of current and former employees for recovery of back wages under the Unfair Competition Law ("UCL") under Columbia Business Code Section 17200. In a class action, a plaintiff, in a representative capacity, seeks recovery on behalf of other persons. "A plaintiff seeking to maintain a class action under the Unfair Competition Law must satisfy the stringent requirements for showing community of interest among the represented parties, common issues of law and fact, adequate representation of the class interests by the nominal parties, and sufficient numerosity." *Arentz v. Angelina Dairy.*

In order for a private plaintiff to bring a representative action under Unfair Competition Law, he must meet standing requirements of 17204 and comply with section 382. (*Arentz*). Section 17203 states "Any person may pursue representative claims or relief on behalf of others only if the claimant meets the standing requirements of Section 17204 and complies with Section 382 of the Code of Procedure."

Required Elements under Section 17204

Plaintiff must meet requirements of Section 17204. To meet this, he must have "suffered injury in fact and has lost money or property as a result of unfair competition." Unfair competition is defined as "any unlawful, unfair or fraudulent business act or practice" (Section 17200). Plaintiff alleges violations of Columbia Labor Code Sections 201, 203, 226.7, and 510, which are probably sufficient to satisfy the requirement of injury in fact and lost money as a result of fraudulent business acts.

Required Elements under Section 382

Class actions in the State of Columbia are authorized under Section 382 of the Columbia Code of Procedure ("Columbia Code"). In *Campbell v. Omnibus Industries,* the Columbia Supreme Court held that Section 382 is to be "applied and interpreted in the same way as Rule 23 of the Federal Rules of Civil Procedure is applied to class actions brought in the federal courts." (*Westlund v. Palladin Farms).* Section 382 states that "when the question is one of a common or general interest, of many persons, or when the parties are numerous, and it is impracticable to bring them all before the court, one or more may sue or defend for the benefit of all."

Rule 23 prescribes the following basic essentials for the maintenance of class actions:

(i)   Numerosity: The class is so numerous that joinder of all members is impracticable;

(ii)   Commonality: There are questions of law or fact common to the case;

(iii)   Typicality: The claims or defenses of the representative parties are typical of the claims or defenses of the class; and

(iv)   Adequacy of Representation: The representative will fairly and adequately protect the interests of the class.

In order to meet the requirements for class certification under the Unfair Competition Law, as outlined in Section 382 of the Columbia Code, all four elements must be established. Because "a party seeking certification of a class bears the burden of establishing that there is an ascertainable class and a well-defined community of interest among the class members," our client would bear this burden. (*Arentz v. Angelina Dairy*).

I. Numerosity

Whether numerosity element is met depends on whether the class is so numerous that it would be impracticable to make each member assert a separate claim. Section 382 refers to this as "of many persons."

In *Westlund*, the plaintiff was attempting to certify of approximately 225 members. About 150 were field workers while 75 were packing house workers. Some of these workers were employed for the entirely of each of the harvests, while others were employed for varying periods of time. The court found that this was sufficient to satisfy the numerosity requirement.

Similarly, according to our client Mr. Wong, Pavlik averages about 350-400 wage earners a year working. Although he noted that there is a lot of turnover, this will probably be sufficient to meet the numerosity requirement. There are in fact more employees than there were in *Westlund*, and like in *Westlund*, the high turnover rates suggest that these employees are employed for varying periods of time. Finally, Mr. Wong believes that many of the employees are in the country illegally. It is unclear from the relevant case law whether this would be a factor to consider in asserting the claim, although under *Talbott* he may be able to use discovery to ascertain this information.

Thus, the 350-400 wage earners at Pavlik will probably satisfy the numerosity requirement.

II. Commonality

The second prong of the four-part test is commonality. In order to satisfy this test, there must be questions of law or fact common to the case. As Section 382 states, the question must be one of a common or general interest.

In *Westlund*, the court found that the "kinds of wage violations alleged vary from group to group within the proposed class and the fundamental components necessary to establish the violations are likely to vary from individual to individual." To begin with, the plaintiff was the only salaried employee in the proposed class. He alleged that the defendant unlawfully withheld portions of his weekly salary purportedly to cover expenses for rental and meals furnished to him. On the other hand, the other employees in the class were not salaried employees: some were packing house workers and others were field workers. The claims he asserted on behalf of the field workers was that defendant routinely short-counted the piecework chits submitted, thus depriving them of payments for varying amount of crops picked and turned in. He also asserted on behalf of the packing workers that some were paid less than the minimum wage and some were not paid for time spent at the beginning of each shift assembling and otherwise preparing crates for the packing process and at the end of each shift cleaning up their work areas.

There appeared to be four main problems with the plaintiff in *Westlund*'s attempt to certify the class: (i) he was a salaried employee and all others in the claim were non-salaried employees, (ii) the claims he was asserting (withholding portions of weekly salary), were separate and distinct from the claims he was asserting on behalf of the others, (iii) even with the others, the violations varied between field workers and packing workers, (iv) even within those claims, there didn't appear to be consistency (i.e., some packing workers were paid less than minimum wage while others were not). As a result, the court denied class certification on the grounds that the commonality requirement was not satisfied. Because the alleged pay practices involved "a wide variety of Labor Code sections and affect different employees in different ways, such that claims are not susceptible of resolution on a class basis," the court was unable to find "that questions of fact and law common to class members predominate[d] over questions of fact and law affecting only individual members" and denied certification.

Because Mr. Wong's case against Pavlik is fairly complicated with many components, in order to assess the likelihood of satisfying the commonality requirement, the different claims being asserted will be distinguished.

Mr. Wong's claims:

    1.   He received no lunch break pay (Section **226.7** - "one hour's extra pay due for each missed meal period").

    2.   He was never paid overtime like the law requires (Section **510** - "requirement to pay time and one-half for overtime after 8 hours a day or 40 hours a week").

    3.   He was not paid for work prior to termination after termination (Section **201** - "failure to pay all wages due upon discharge from employment"; possibly Section **203** - "additional wages up to 30 day's pay for violation of Section 201").

Claim that generally affected all the hourly workers:

    1.   Pavlik would not give them pay stubs that explained their pay (Section **226** - "requirement for pay stubs showing hours, rate of pay, and wage calculation").

Claims within the potential class that some employees had while others did not:

    1.   Some workers, mostly cleanup crew, were paid less than the minimum wage (Section **1194** - "failure to pay minimum wage").

    2.   Most workers, excluding generally the butchers, did not get paid overtime and almost everyone worked overtime (Section **510** - "requirement to

pay time and one-half for overtime after 8 hours a day or 40 hours a week").

3.   "A lot of" people never got their final pay (Section **201** - "failure to pay all wages due upon discharge from employment"; possibly Section **203** - "additional wages up to 30 day's pay for violation of Section 201").

4.   Sometimes Pavlik would pay some terminated employees in cash about half of what they were really owed and make them sign a release before giving them the money (Section **206.5** - "unlawful to require release from employee as a condition to receiving wages due").

5.   Some workers got time off for lunch while others did not (Section **512** - "requirement for meal period of specified length during work shift").

There does not appear to be a cut-and-dry answer for whether the court would, given the facts stipulated above, find that this satisfies the commonality requirement. The one claim that generally affected all the hourly workers-- Section 226--does not seem to be at issue for Mr. Wong. In addition, there are numerous claims that affect some of the potential class that do not affect Mr. Wong (Sections 512, 206.5, 1194). On the other hand, at least "most workers", including Mr. Wong, seem to be affected by Section 510. Additionally, "a lot of" people, including Mr. Wong, seem to be affected by Section 210. The last consideration is that only Mr. Wong seems to be affected by Section 226.7.

Unlike *Westland*, there appears to be more consistency in our present case, to the point where the court might find that there is a common question of law or fact common to the class.

Given the complexity and number of matters regarding wage practices involved, this would ultimately be a question for the court. However, *Talbott* established that the "plaintiff should at least have the opportunity to produce the evidence, at which time the question of the merits can be tested." It is possible that through discovery, Mr. Wong might meet the burden of proof needed to satisfy this element.

Appears that Wong is hourly too (paid fifteen dollars an hour")

III. Typicality

To satisfy the third prong of the test, a plaintiff must show that his claims are typical of the types of claims he asserts on behalf of the other members of the proposed class.

As outlined above, in *Westlund*, the plaintiff's claims were not typical of the types of claims he was trying to assert on behalf of the other members. He was a salaried employee while the others were not. Furthermore, his claims regarded improperly withheld portions of his weekly salary, while the other claims in the class varied from field workers being deprived payments for crops they turned in, to some packing workers being paid less than minimum wage, to some packing workers not being paid for time spent assembling and cleaning. Thus, the court found that the typicality requirement was not satisfied.

As discussed above, our case is quite complicated with many elements. However, unlike *Westlund* where there were no claims sufficiently common between the plaintiff and the asserted class, at least "most workers", including Mr. Wong, seem to be affected by Section 510. Additionally, "a lot of" people, including Mr. Wong, seem to be affected by Section 210. Thus, our case can probably be distinguished from *Westlund*, where no claims were common.

IV. Adequacy of Representation

To satisfy the fourth requirement, a plaintiff must show that the representative parties will fairly and adequately protect the interests of the class. Section 382 states that "one or more may sue or defend for the benefit of all." While it does not explicitly address adequacy, since the Supreme Court held that Section 382 should be applied and interpreted the same way as Rule 23 of the Federal Rules of Civil Procedure, it is safe to presume that this requirement is implied within the language.

In *Westlund*, the court found that because the plaintiff's claims were not at all typical of the claims he asserted on behalf of the other members of the proposed class, he would not have been able to fairly and adequately represent the diverse interests of the proposed class members.

The more typical the claims within a class are and between plaintiff, the more likely a court will find adequacy of representation. As discussed under typicality, sections 510 and 210 seem to be typical among the class. Additionally, Wong seems eager to "get them their money too if there's any way to do it." He had also spoken up numerous times to Pavlik about the disparities, and "that's what started this whole thing because I was speaking up for them." He seems ready to "sue or defend for the benefit of all."

Thus, we have a strong case that Mr. Wong would be an adequate representative for the class as a whole.

Talbott established that Plaintiff can conduct discovery on class actions. It found that "whether the class claims lack merit is a question of fact based on the proof that Plaintiff might be able to bring to bear once the identity and circumstances of the members are determined." Thus, Mr. Wong would likely be able to conduct discovery to strengthen his claims.

PRIVATE ATTORNEY GENERAL ACT [COLUMBIA LABOR CODE SECTION 2699]

We have a strong argument that Mr. Wong can bring a representative claim under PAGA on back wages without having to satisfy class certification requirements. The question involves two prongs: whether Mr. Wong can bring a representative claim under PAGA without having to satisfy class certification requirements, and whether Mr. Wong can bring a representative claim under

PAGA on back wages. The requirements for bringing a PAGA are set forth under Labor Code Section 2699.3, explained further below.

No Class Certification Requirements Satisfaction Required for PAGA Claim

The court in *Arentz* held that "a plaintiff may maintain a representative action under PAGA to recover civil penalties without having to satisfy the traditional requirements for certification of a class." Thus, Mr. Wong does not have to satisfy any class certification requirements in order to bring a PAGA claim.

"Under this legislation, an 'aggrieved employee' may bring a civil action personally and on behalf of other current or former employees to recover civil penalties for Labor Code violations." (*Arentz*). This is because it is in the public interest to allow aggrieved employees, acting as private attorneys general, to recover civil penalties for Labor Code violations. The reason is that the labor law enforcement agencies simply do not have the staffing, financing or capacity to deal with every single labor code violation. By allowing private individuals to bring such cases, essentially as proxies of the enforcement agencies, it benefits the public interest: more aggrieved employees will have their claims addressed and hopefully cured. As discussed below under "Additional Questions," the recovery goes 75% to the labor agency with 25% going to aggrieved employees.

The appeals court in the *Arentz* case relied on three reasons in determining that Plaintiff does not need to satisfy the class action certification requirements:
1. Labor Code Section 2699(a) states that "notwithstanding any other provision of law" an aggrieved employee may bring an action against the employer "on behalf of himself...and other current or former employees."
2. Unlike UCL's Section 17203, the PAGA does not expressly require that the representative actions comply with Section 382.
3. A private plaintiff suing under this act is essentially bringing a law enforcement action designed to protect the public.

Given these three reasons and the court's ruling in *Arentz*, Mr. Wong will not have to satisfy the class certification requirements.

PAGA Can Be Used For Claim on Back Wages

The question arose in *Talbott* whether the PAGA authorizes only for statutory penalties or for civil penalties as well. The question in that case was whether one could bring a representative suit for civil penalties under PAGA can also maintain, in the same action, claims for unpaid wages for members of the class he purports to represent. The Court of Appeals held that the trial court misapprehended this question of first impression when the trial court dismissed Plaintiff's PAGA claim for the recovery of unpaid wages on behalf of the class.

There are good claims on both sides of this argument. On one hand, it can be argued that the Act authorizes a representative action "only for the purpose of seeking statutory penalties for Labor Code violations," quoting the language of the court in *Arentz*. The argument is that anything other than civil penalties, such as unpaid wages, are not penalties so they cannot be a component of any PAGA recovery.

On the other hand, Labor Code Section 2699(d) states that "Nothing in this part shall operate to limit an employee's right to pursue or recover other remedies available under state law or federal law, either separately or concurrently with an action taken under this part." The argument could be made that "other remedies" includes unpaid wages. This, in conjunction with Labor Code Section 558, which allows the Labor Commissioner, who is head of the Division of Labor Standards, to issue citations for recovery of both unpaid wages and civil penalties, seems to create a strong argument that back wages would be able to be recovered under a PAGA claim. It states that "wages recovered pursuant to this section shall be paid to the affected employee." In concluding the case, the Plaintiff argued that "the logical conclusion to be drawn from the combination of Section 2699(d) and Section 558 is that PAGA provides private individuals, standing in the shoes of the state labor law enforcement agencies, the representative action mechanism to recover unpaid wages through private enforcement of Section 558."

While the court in *Talbott* did not come to a definite conclusion, but rather stated that the "trial court misapprehended this question of first impression" and remanded to the trial court, it seems likely that if we tried to recover back wages under a PAGA claim, we would have a strong case for doing so. The only thing that would act against us is the court's statement in *Arentz* that "the Act authorizes a representative action only for the purpose of seeking statutory penalties for Labor Code violations, and an action to recover civil penalties is fundamentally a law enforcement action designed to protect the public and not to benefit private parties." The language that it is "not to benefit private parties" obviously weighs strongly against us. *Talbott* is also a Court of Appeals decision while *Arentz* is a Supreme Court decision. However, we could argue that this language is not essential to the holding in *Arentz*, and instead is simply dicta that is not binding. Thus, despite the language that weighs against our favor in *Arentz*, we could probably still argue based on what is outlined above and the supporting language in *Talbott* that PAGA can be used for claim on back wages.

In conclusion, because the court in *Arentz* "held that a plaintiff may maintain a representative action under PAGA to recover civil penalties without having to satisfy the traditional requirements for certification of a class." (*Talbott*). Additionally, if we are able to prove that PAGA authorizes back wages, we could succeed in a PAGA claim.

The Effect of a PAGA Judgment

A PAGA judgment binds not only the employee but also state labor law enforcement agencies. It also binds nonparty aggrieved employees. This is because the aggrieved employee's action functions as a substitute for an action brought by the government itself, and nonparty aggrieved employees would be bound by a judgment in an action brought by the government. Nonparty employees can use collateral estoppel to obtain remedies other than civil penalties. So there is a potential for nonparty aggrieved employees to benefit from a favorable judgment under PAGA.

Additional Questions Regarding Monetary Relief

Regarding the specific questions about monetary relief we can obtain, please refer to the answers that follow.

(a) Under the UCL, the Attorney General may recover civil penalties. Section 17206 provides that "any person who engages, has engaged, or proposes to engage in unfair competition shall be liable for a civil penalty not to exceed $2,500 for each violation, which shall be assessed and recovered in a civil action brought in the name of the people of the State of Columbia by the Attorney General."

(b) Under PAGA, the prerequisites that need to be satisfied before filing suit are governed by Labor Code Section 2699.3 and also outlined by the court in *Arentz*. An employee must give written notice by certified mail of the alleged Labor Code violations to both the employer and the Labor and Workforce Development Agency, and the notice must describe facts and theories supporting the violation as well as the specific provisions of the code alleged to have been violated. Second, the agency shall notify the employer and the aggrieved employee or representative that it does not intend to investigate the alleged violation within 30 calendar days of the postmark date of the notice. If the agency notifies the employee and the employer that it does not intend to investigate, or if the agency fails to respond within 33 days, the employee may then bring a civil action against the employer pursuant to Section 2699.

(c) Under PAGA, employees do not get to keep all the civil penalties we might recover. Instead, pursuant to Section 2699(e), civil penalties recovered by aggrieved employees shall be distributed as follows: 75% to the Labor and

Workforce Development Agency for enforcement of labor laws, and 25% to the aggrieved employees. The rationale behind this is that an employee suing is acting as a proxy or agent of the state's labor enforcement agencies; thus the employee plaintiff represents the same legal right and interest as state labor law enforcement agencies--namely, recovery of civil penalties that otherwise would have been assessed and collected by the Labor Workforce Development Agency. (*Arentz*).